Northern Virginia Association for History, Inc.

P.O. BOX 1366 • FAIRFAX, VIRGINIA 22030

The Northern Virginia Association for History, Inc., an umbrella organization of individuals and societies seeking to increase public appreciation of Northern Virginia's history, is fortunate to have the opportunity to enthusiastically endorse the book, *This Was Virginia 1900–1927 As Shown By The Glass Negatives Of J. Harry Shannon, the Rambler.*

The prints of the glass negatives include views of nationally known historic Virginia sites as well as locally prominent houses, mills, churches, etc., some no longer standing. Usually accompanying each photograph in the way of explanation is a caption excerpted from Mr. Shannon's own Washington *Sunday Star* articles. Annotations by the author are added where appropriate. In this way, historical, genealogical and topographical information relating to the photos is imparted to the readers.

The broad scope covered by the prints (to the far points of Fredericksburg, Appomattox, Montross, Leesburg, Harrisonburg, Bull Run) makes this a very pleasant and accurate way to review the history of the northern part of Virginia.

For these reasons, the Board of Directors of the Northern Virginia Association for History, Inc. believes our endorsement of this book project will promote interest in Northern Virginia's history. This permanent record of J. Harry Shannon's photography will be of lasting cultural and educational value to the people of Virginia and the Nation.

HALLMARK

This Was Virginia 1900 – 1927

As Shown by the Glass Negatives of J. Harry Shannon, The Rambler

Connie Pendleton Stuntz
Mayo Sturdevant Stuntz

Dedicated To

Our daughter

Grace Barton Stuntz (1948–1950)

and

Our two youngest grandchildren

Katherine Anne Cohn Stuntz

Stephen Fitzhugh Stuntz Swanson

Hallmark Publishing Company, Inc.
P.O. Box 901
Gloucester Point, VA 23062–0901

B. L. Walton Jr., President/Publisher
Lynn Walton, Vice President/Production
Sally Davis, Editor
Kevin Brown, Graphic Designer

Library of Congress Cataloging-in-Publication Data

Stuntz, Connie Pendleton.
        This was Virginia, 1900–1927 : as shown by the glass negatives of
    J. Harry Shannon, the Rambler / Connie Pendleton Stuntz, Mayo
    Sturdevant Stuntz.
                        p.   cm.
        Includes index.
        ISBN 0–9653759–7–8 (hardcover : alk. paper)
        1. Virginia—History—20th century—Pictorial works. 2. Virginia—
    Description and travel. 3. Shannon, J. Harry, 1869–1928—Journeys—
    Virginia. I. Shannon, J. Harry, 1869–1928. II. Stuntz, Mayo S.
    III. Title.
    F231.S92 1998
    975.5'041—dc21   98–46162
                                                              CIP

Table of Contents

Acknowledgements

J. Harry Shannon: Of course, our biggest debt of gratitude is to Mr. J. Harry Shannon (The Rambler) for his diligent effort in recording our Virginia heritage. He would be pleased with our effort to present the prints of his glass negatives to new generations. He might even agree with the accompanying selections from his corresponding articles that appeared in the *Sunday Star,* though I'm sure he'd think them too abbreviated.

Anne Stuntz Swanson: When we were mulling over the final destination of our glass negative collection, our daughter, in a telephone call from England, asked, "Why don't you publish them?" It seemed like a simple process then.

Gale Youman: The first person to send us on our way toward this publication was Gale Youman, a transplanted Australian, who professionally developed our five hundred Rambler glass negatives way below the charge asked by his commercial competitors.

Bonnie Hedges, Gail Redmann, Jack Brewer: A visit to the library of the Historical Society of Washington, D.C., from whence our glass negative collection had come, was next on our agenda. The then librarian, Bonnie Hedges, introduced us to the Rambler file in which we found record of some Virginia glass negatives not included in our 1967 purchase. Her successor, Gail Redmann, made it possible for us to obtain prints of those we thought important additions to our collection. We appreciate the time and assistance given us by them and by Jack Brewer, a long-time volunteer in the library.

Suzanne Levy, Anita Ramos, Brian Conley, John K. Gott, Orlo C. Paciulli: Then it was time to scan the Rambler's 1912–1927 *Sunday Star* articles which are on microfilm in the Virginia Room at the Fairfax City Regional Library in Fairfax, Virginia. Many hours were spent at a microfilm reader with the ready help of the library staff at all times. Brian Conley alerted us to the bound typed copy of some of the Rambler's articles made by John K. Gott which relieved the burdensome reading of early microfilm. As did the copies Orlo C. Paciulli, III had xeroxed of some of the other Rambler articles.

Malcolm Richardson: Later when Malcolm Richardson's index of all the Rambler series was published, it was a pleasure to confirm our findings and add information from his thorough effort.

Scot Boatright: As with our Tysons book, Scot helped us with his photographic talent by reproducing the Rambler prints located in the Fairfax City Regional Library.

Mary Burke Wood: Because my husband, Mayo, can no longer type my manuscripts due to macular degeneration, our long time Vienna friend, Mary Burke Wood, took on the task. She did a magnificent job with nary a complaint when revisions and additions had to be made to the final draft. Thank you, Mary, for keeping our dream alive.

John K. Gott: Asking someone to read one's manuscript for comments is tricky for both writer and reader, but John Gott, an author in his own right and well-known Northern Virginia historian, kindly encouraged us just enough, and added pertinent information for which we are very grateful.

Edith Moore Sprouse: The manuscript was also read by another well-versed area historian and writer, Edith Moore Sprouse. She is the one I mention in the first chapter as introducing us to articles written by J. Harry Shannon before the 1912 start of his Rambler series. She, too, refined some of my aside comments to Mr. Shannon's articles. We are most appreciative of her well-documented references.

Brian Conley: Another person with wide historic interests and knowledge in and of the area, Brian Conley, Assistant Librarian in the Virginia Room of the library in Fairfax, was kind enough to read the manuscript. His additions and confirmation of the worth of this production were very beneficial.

Amy Thompson: And finally, it was a pleasure doing business with Amy Thompson of Business Images in Vienna. Her copying work of our preliminary material and manuscripts was always A-One.

Fig. I-1
"The Rambler"
J. Harry Shannon
(1869–1928)

Mr. Shannon, the journalist/photographer who is the illustrious man we pay homage to in the following chapters, was born 3 April 1869 in Baltimore, Maryland. His early boyhood years, however, were spent in Anacostia, District of Columbia. As a boy, natural history and collecting relics were interests that remained with him throughout his lifetime. Another early interest, noted and appreciated in the 22 October 1880 *Alexandria Gazette,* was oration: "J. Harry Shannon, the boy orator, will give an exhibit of his wonderful elocutionary powers at Amory Hall tonight. The Press of the country speak to the highest terms of the boy and the entertainments given by him. The Philadelphia press says: 'He renders the thoughts of the most eminent writers with a dignity and eloquence which cannot be surpassed.' Among the selections tonight will be 'Lees Farewell to The Army.'"[1]

Chapter I

Introducing the Contributions
of J. Harry Shannon

The purpose of this book is to show the public the prints developed from the glass negatives (dry plates) made by John Harry Shannon on his treks into Virginia between 1900–1927.

A reporter for the *Evening Star* from 1890 to 1895 and a member of its editorial staff from 1900 to his demise on 12 February 1928, J. Harry Shannon earned his famous nom de plume, "The Rambler," after his series of weekly articles, illustrated by his own photographs, began appearing in the *Sunday Star* in 1912. His widely read Rambler articles reported Mr. Shannon's "rambles" through his home base of Washington, D.C., and neighboring Maryland and Virginia from 1912 to 1922. After a two year lapse due to illness, they resumed from 1924 to 1927. The first title of his articles was: "With the Rambler in Odd Nooks and Crannies about the City," which gave way to "With the Rambler" from 7 June 1914. From 6 August 1916 onward, his articles were entitled, "The Rambler Writes of . . .," "The Rambler Visits . . .," or "The Rambler Discovers. . . ."

Before the start of his Rambler series in 1912, unsigned articles in earlier *Sunday Star* editions were located by Edith Moore Sprouse, a local historian who twenty years ago while perusing the *Star* microfilm at the Martin Luther King Library in Washington, D.C., noted the similarity to the Rambler's style with accompanying photographs. When she reviewed my manuscript, she brought to our attention this fact. And proof

that most of the unsigned articles, in which the author sometimes identified himself as the "Star Man," are indeed the work of J. Harry Shannon was then verified when we found some of our early Rambler prints matched those in the articles. The earliest exact match was in the 7 May 1905, Part 4, p. 6, *Sunday Star* in an article entitled, "Belvoir and Its Departed Glory." Two of the four or five photos exhibited were copies from our glass negatives, the originals of the others perhaps destroyed. According to Mrs. Sprouse and information from Bob Levey's *Washington Post* researcher, the *Sunday Star* edition of the *Evening Star* began on 26 March 1905.

Our obvious conclusion then is that Mr. Shannon wrote articles about historic sites beginning at least in 1905 using his early negatives to illustrate them. As I found after scanning a few articles at the Martin Luther King Library, a lot of the information contained therein was repeated in his later Rambler series.

Usually on foot (if the distance from Washington City was too great he used the steam or electric railway or the steamboat down the Potomac, and then walked) and carrying his camera, tripod, supply of glass plates, notebook and perhaps his lunch, he recorded his keen observations by word and by picture which formed the basis of his writings. The description of churches, graveyards, old homes and their families, battlefields, and the roads he traveled to reach them in the early 1900s are written in a pleasant conversational style, obviously by someone in easy command of the English language. Very evident to the reader is the extensive historical and genealogical research done by the Rambler. His vast knowledge of the topography of the region and his familiarity with the various forms of local vegetation are also abundantly clear. All these attributes made his articles popular with thousands of readers, most of whom knew him only as "The Rambler."

When the glass negatives he had amassed on his excursions were donated to the Columbia Historical Society, the forerunner of the Historical Society of Washington, D.C., in the mid 1960s, they numbered approximately 1,800. The Rambler's own words found in his 24 January 1914 *Sunday Star* article describe the size of his collection:

The Rambler has collected thousands of pictures and has great piles of those things which photographers know as 'negatives.' The heaps of glass sometimes look to him like junk. The tons of negatives interfere with orderly housekeeping, but it is hard to part with them. Only a small percentage of these pictures have ever appeared in a newspaper. The Rambler looks on those as personal souvenirs and relics and not as objects of business. Every time he puts his hands into these piles of negatives he draws out one that brings up recollections of a trip—perhaps a laborious and weary trip, perhaps a gladsome sort of fairy trip. The road might have been cold, bleak and dreary, and deep in mud; it might have been blister-hot and ankle-deep in choking dust, or it might have been a road lined with roses and apple blossoms.[2]

My husband, Mayo S. Stuntz, and I bought part of the Rambler collection of glass negatives, more properly known as "dry plate negatives," thirty years ago, the part that pertained to the northern section of Virginia.[3] The opportunity arose when Miss Josephine Cobb, in charge of Still Photographs at the National Archives, was also heavily involved in working with photos at the Columbia Historical Society. The Society, wishing to limit its Rambler collection to the District of Columbia and needing funds to develop said negatives, planned to sell the Rambler's collection of Virginia. Miss Cobb, who was a friend and fellow member of the Landmarks Preservation Committee of Fairfax County, the predecessor of the Fairfax History Commission, offered the Virginia part of the Rambler's glass negatives to Mayo. She was acutely aware of his hobby of collecting photos of Northern Virginia. Reiterated by her that the offer was made by the Columbia Historical Society to Mayo as an individual, he and I agreed to pay one dollar each—only to find there were approximately five hundred of them. Although the Rambler articles began in 1912, many of our glass negatives date earlier, between 1900 and 1912.

For those of you who have questions about the glass negative or dry plate negative, I have gathered the following information.

"Dry plate negative: Historically speaking, the dry plate was sandwiched in between the wet-collodion method of photography, on a heavy glass plate, and the early production of film for the camera. The dry plate became commercially available around 1880, and even after the introduction of film and its close-to-universal use, the dry plate still had its advocates until around 1920. The dry plate glass negative can be recognized by its relative thinness and its lightness, its sharp edges, and the relative smoothness of its coating."[4]

The predecessor of the dry plate, the wet-collodion plate process, was invented in 1851, and by 1860 had surpassed its predecessor, the by then out-moded daguerreotype, a direct image on silver-plated copper invented in 1839.[5] Different from the later dry plate used by the Rambler, the thicker glass plate in the wet plate method was coated with a solution of collodion by the photographer himself. Then the coated plate was sensitized in a bath of silver nitrate, put in a dark slide, carried to the camera, exposed, and immediately developed in a portable darkroom, all while the emulsion was still wet and all in one continuous action.[6]

The emergence of the dry plate negative simplified the art of taking pictures for the photographer. These commercially manufactured glass plates were

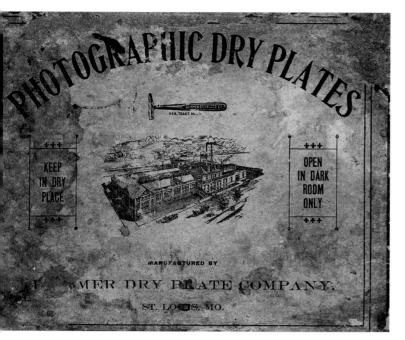

Fig. I-2
From the cover of a box of dry plates.

precoated and presensitized in the factory. The "silver image carried in a layer of gelatin on a sheet of glass (was) capable of maintaining its chemical sensitivity to light over long storage periods before use. The glass plate, coated with the gelatin containing light-sensitive silver bromide, was sold to photographers ready for use. In the darkroom an unexposed plate was loaded into a plate holder to be exposed in the camera as needed. Exposed plates were brought back to the darkroom to be developed, fixed, washed and dried."[7]

To explain further, according to John Gott, a local historian who remembers his yearly school pictures being taken by a photographer using dry plates, each unexposed plate was encased, in a darkroom, in a small thin metal container called the "plate holder" or "sleeve" to protect it from light. When the plate was placed in the camera, a spring was pressed releasing the glass plate from the plate holder. After exposure, while still in the camera, the plate was slipped back into the holder before removal, then only to be released from the holder in the darkroom.

Although the dry plate came ready for use for the camera freeing the photographer of some of the burdensome procedures, the Rambler's monumental efforts in the early 1900s are to be appreciated and admired. His first exploratory trek to Westmoreland County in the fall of 1903 confirms his indomitable spirit and devotion to his new project: *"Walked to Potomac Mills and got to the hotel at Montross—a walk of something like 25 miles with a heavy camera and two dozen plates."*

In 1967, we received our 5 x 7 Rambler dry glass negatives from the Columbia Historical Society in separate manila folders, each of which was very briefly identified by Mr. Shannon, usually giving its geographical locale or historical connection, a specific designation and often a date. This has been faithfully reproduced in italics with each photo. Any bracketed information under the pictures and in the text is from sources other than the Rambler. The text written in italics is directly quoted from his newspaper articles. Fuller information about the prints can be located in the

Fig. I-3
The Rambler's camera was similar to this Eastman View No. 2 "Improved model of Century View and Empire State No. 2, Eastman Kodak, Rochester, New York, U.S.A." (This is a photo of Bill Harrah's antique camera he had used successfully in years past in his Wolf Run Studio).

11

corresponding Rambler articles which are available on microfilm in some local libraries.

In 1947, The Columbia Historical Society published in its yearbook a topical index of all the Rambler's articles.[8] Back in 1924 and 1930 the Washington Public Library (now the Martin Luther King Library) in conjunction with the *Evening Star* Newspaper Company, bound the Rambler's articles in four over-sized scrapbooks. In time these disintegrated and were discarded by the Library, but not before the articles were microfilmed. Just recently an exhaustive index to the complete set of Rambler articles was prepared by Malcolm L. Richardson of Fairfax County and is available in the Virginia Room at the Fairfax City Regional Library in Fairfax, Virginia, and in the library of the Historical Society of Washington, D.C.

In 1995, as we looked through our collection of glass negatives by the Rambler in preparation for their future stability and security, the beautiful photography with tremendous historical value seemed very worthy of broad exposure. The realization that it was our responsibility to give J. Harry Shannon's glass negatives that exposure spurred us on to make this publication effort.

Assembling our geographically disparate prints of the glass negatives of Virginia in some semblance of order so that they could be displayed in the most meaningful manner was a problem to be reckoned with. My solution was to begin at the Aqueduct Bridge (replaced by Key Bridge after 1923) between Georgetown and Rosslyn as the Rambler often did, and go southward to Fredericksburg, thereby including Arlington Cemetery, Mount Vernon, Gunston Hall, Pohick Church and other spots of great historical interest along the way. From Fredericksburg I continued southeast to cover the Rambler's travels to George Washington's birthplace "Wakefield," "Stratford Hall," Montross, to name a few. Also from Fredericksburg, a Rambler's journey touched Chancellorsville, Appomattox, and finally Yorktown. Next I went back up north to Chain Bridge to go northwest by the Georgetown Leesburg Pike (Route 193) to

its meeting place with Route 7 near the Dranesville Tavern, then on Route 7 to Leesburg and on to Harpers Ferry, Harrisonburg and Front Royal. Then I jumped back to old Route 123 at Langley and proceeded through Tysons Corner, Vienna, Fairfax to Centreville, etc. Not all of the Rambler's photos fit on these beaten paths. When that happened, I placed the print as strategically as possible.

Unfortunately, our collection does not include all of the Rambler's Virginia plates. To help remedy this and to make his treks more complete, we were able to use some prints of his Virginia glass negatives remaining in the care of the Historical Society of Washington, D.C. We also added a few pertinent Rambler prints in the possession of the Fairfax County Public Library Photographic Archive. The Gelman Library at George Washington University, Washington, D.C., also has some Virginia glass negatives of Mr. Shannon's of which we reproduced one, the others being duplicates of our collection. Even with these additions, some of the photos published in the Rambler's articles are missing, the glass negatives supposedly destroyed. We were informed that sometimes the used negatives were retained by the *Evening Star* for a short period, then discarded.[9]

Because I usually quote only the Rambler's words relating to the accumulated prints, many worthy sites mentioned in his articles are excluded. However, the following multitudinous examples of the Rambler's photography in conjunction with his articles are still an excellent authentic source of 'the way it was' in this northern section of Virginia in the early 1900s.

Connie Stuntz

Photographic Credits

References are to photograph numbers in the text.

The Historical Society of Washington, D. C.,
Rambler Collection
> Chapter II–2, 2a, 6, 7, 8, 9
> Chapter IV–4a
> Chapter VI–1a, 49a, 66, 67
> Chapter VIII–11, 18, 18a

Fairfax County Public Library Photographic Archive
> Chapter III–2, 18a
> Chapter VI–4, 10, 11, 13, 58
> Chapter VIII–1a, 3, 9

George Washington University, Gelman Library,
Charles Kelly Collection
> Chapter III–3a

Bureau of Public Roads, National Archives
> Chapter VI–8a

Notes on Chapter I

1. Located by John K. Gott.
2. Abstracted by M. L. Richardson 2-4-96.
3. In our collection were a few Washington, D.C., and Maryland glass negatives which we recently presented to the Historical Society of Washington, D.C.
4. Margaret Haller, *Collecting Old Photographs*, Arco Publishing Co., Inc., New York, 1978, p. 24.
5. Ibid pp. 23, 24.
6. John Hannavy, *Masters of Victorian Photography*, Holmes and Meier Publishers, Inc., New York, 1976, p. 26.
7. Robert A. Weinstein and Larry Booth, *Collection, Use, and Care of Historical Photographs*, American Association for State and Local History, Nashville, Tennessee, 1977, p. 177.
8. *Records of the Columbia Historical Society*, Washington, D.C., Volume 46–47, 1947, pp. 130–212.
9. By word of James Birchfield (1908–1997), a *Washington Star* editor and columnist who also worked on the "picture desk." He retired from The *Star* in 1974.

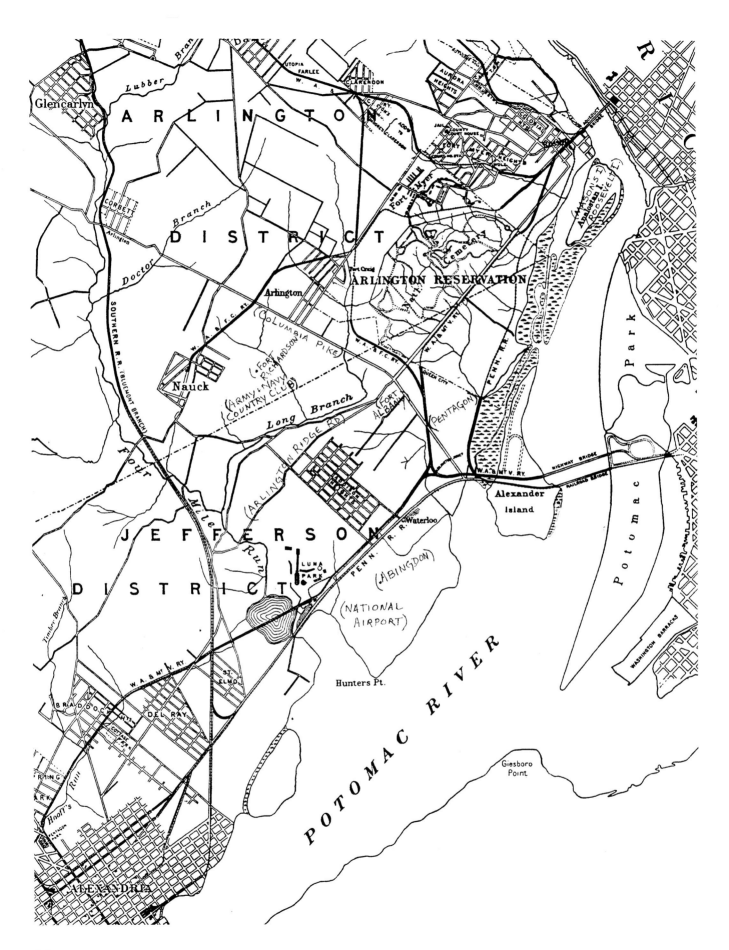

PART 1. DOWN THE RIVER

Chapter II

Following His Treks Southward
from Washington, D.C.

The Rambler, J. Harry Shannon, began his treks into Virginia from his home and work place in Washington, D.C. Often he would cross the Potomac River by the Aqueduct Bridge which connected Georgetown to Rosslyn, Virginia. The present Key Bridge replaced it in 1923.

Left: II-1
*1907 Gregor Noetzel Map of Alexandria County, Virginia
(Arlington County) with additions in parenthesis*

II-2
*Aqueduct Bridge and Key Bridge [under construction],
Georgetown, D.C., 1921*

The story of the Aqueduct Bridge is found in the following excerpts from the Rambler's 17 August 1912 article: . . . *the old canal which separated from the main stem of the Chesapeake and Ohio Canal at Georgetown, crossed the Potomac by means of the Aqueduct Bridge, passed southward through the low lands east of Arlington (the National Cemetery) . . . and entered the Potomac River above Alexandria.*

The water was let out of the aqueduct in 1861, and it was used by marching columns of Union troops.

. . . *Congress made an appropriation in 1886 of $240,000 for the purchase of and reconstruction of the bridge as a free bridge and it was opened to travel March 31, 1888.*

The following is from the Rambler's 9 November 1924 article: *The Aqueduct is in the news today because its superstructure is being taken down and money is being asked of Congress at its next session to remove the piers. The new bridge, the Free Bridge as the Citizens Committee has named it, was a thing of beauty in the morning sun. It stretched in graceful lines to the Virginia shore.*

II-2a
Aqueduct Bridge 1924

II-3

Group above Rosslyn

13 February 1921: *A jagged line of grey rocks reaches from Analostan Island to the Rosslyn shore. Seen from the Aqueduct Bridge or from the city streets that are high above the north end of the bridge, you think that it is a narrow line or ledge of tumbled rocks which links the island and Virginia.*

27 February 1921: *The ruin of the house, the west wall of which is standing, the mounds of debris, the massive foundations, walls and the deep wide cellars show that it was one of the great houses of this part of the world.*

II-4

Analostan Island [now known as Roosevelt Island] *Ruin of Mason House 1920* [More information is found in unsigned *Star* articles for 3 August and 31 August 1907.]

In his 30 January 1921 article, the Rambler quoted the will of George Mason of Gunston, probated in 1792: *I also give and bequeath . . . unto my said son, John Mason . . . my island in Potomac river opposite the mouth of Rock Creek, which I had under a patent from the lord proprietor of Maryland by the name of Barbadoes. . . .* The Rambler goes on to say: *After John Mason built the fine house, the ruins of which may be seen on the island, it came to be generally known as Mason's Island.*

[West southwest of Rosslyn and Mason's Island was located the original court house built on court house hill between Rosslyn and Clarendon in 1898 when Arlington County was still Alexandria County. In 1920, an act changing the name to Arlington was adopted by the General Assembly.][1]

ARLINGTON NATIONAL CEMETERY

Alexandria County Court House 1915, [Becoming Arlington County Court House after 1920.]

In his 27 October 1912 article, the Rambler describes the eastern entrances to the Arlington National Cemetery as they then appeared: *A low red Seneca sandstone wall topped with a thick slab of Potomac bluestone stretches away to the right and left, north and south along the west side of a yellow road dusty or muddy lined with telegraph poles strung with webs of wire and fringed on one side with wild shrubbery now rich and radiant with autumn colors.* [The yellow road was in line of present day Eisenhower Drive . . . the then eastern boundary of the cemetery and the old road that led from the Aqueduct Bridge toward Alexandria. It was called Arlington Ridge Road from the cemetery southward.] *Behind the red stone wall are massed old oaks, white and red, tall shapely cedars, somber spruce. . . . This wall is pierced with a number of gateways, three of them beautiful, the others only utilitarian. The central one of those gateways rises high above the red stone wall. Here swinging on giant hinges are two heavy iron gates, black and gold. . . . The iron gates are flanked on the north and south sides by a wall of Potomac bluestone more than twice as high as the red sandstone wall. On the top of the bluestone wall is a plinth of sandstone and from this rise four sandstone columns coated white. Slightly over half way between base and capital on those columns are names deep cut in stone - the southernmost pillars inscribed 'Scott,' the next 'Lincoln,' the next 'Stanton' and the northernmost pillar 'Grant.' Across the tops of the columns is a heavy establature chiseled with this inscription: 'Six columns erected in the portico of the War Office, Washington, in 1818 were on the demolition of that building in April 1879. They were transferred to the gateways of the Arlington National Cemetery.' Above the establature is a cornice wall transcribed in large letters with the name of 'Sheridan.' Hence this is usually called the Sheridan Gate of Arlington.*

[Just east of the yellow road was the electric trolley line, The Washington, Alexandria, and Mount Vernon Railway.] 27 October 1912: *A two-horse wagon that*

II-6

Sheridan Gate on East Front, 8 December 1918
[The Sheridan Gate is no longer standing but stood just
north of today's massive Memorial Gate.]

*meets electric cars at the Sheridan Gate is driven by a
Horseman.*

27 October 1912: *Follow the yellow road and
the red wall about a quarter of a mile southward and
you stand before a massive monumental red sandstone
gateway. For years this gateway was twisted around
with vines but those have been cut away - the south
column being inscribed . . . Meigs. . . . Above the establature . . . is this in great golden letters, 'McClellan..'*
[This gateway still stands west of the intersection of
Eisenhower Drive and McClellan Drive.]

*The road through this gateway is the original
road into Arlington. It was the road by which the place
was entered when George Washington Parke Custis and
his wife, Mary Fitzhugh, lived there. It was the road
used by Robert E. Lee, his wife and children up to the
time of their departure for Richmond in 1861.*

II-7
McClellan Gate, 8 December 1918

ARLINGTON MANSION

In his 28 March 1915 article, the Rambler outlines *the history of the beautiful place which George Washington Parke Custis and his wife established, which Mrs. Robert E. Lee inherited and which the United States government appropriated and finally, under a decision of the Supreme Court of the U.S. paid for to the heirs of General and Mrs. Lee.*

21 September 1913: *George Washington Parke Custis was the grandson of Mrs. George Washington and ward and adopted son of George Washington . . . [and] a brother of Nellie Custis. He died at 'Arlington' October 10, 1857. The property in 1860 was the home of Robert E. Lee and family, Mrs. Lee having been Ann Randolph Custis, a daughter of Mr. and Mrs. George Washington Parke Custis.*

Arlington House, 8 December 1918

8 December 1918: *It was the residence of Robert E. Lee until 1861 when he resigned his commission in the U.S. Army to join the rebellion . . .* [and Union troops occupied the estate throughout the Civil War.] *By an order of the Secretary of War dated June 15, 1864, the Arlington mansion and the grounds surrounding it, not exceeding 200 acres, were appropriated for a military cemetery. . . .*

II-9

Arlington Mansion and Offices, Side view from Amphitheatre 1913

II-10

Arlington Cemetery, Old Amphitheatre 1913

10 November 1912: *There is an effigy memorial under the bough of the Arlington oaks. . . . Off from the main walk and drive of Arlington in the officers section between the rear of the mansion and the central west gate, there is a large block of dark green marble. . . . On this block of marble is a heavy bronze top and on this top in bronze turned green . . . is the effigy of a soldier representing him as dead . . . stricken on the battlefield. On the east edge of the bronze base of the figure are these words: Lt. John Rodgers Meigs, U.S. Eng'rs, Chief Engineer, Army of the Shenandoah . . . and on the north edge . . . killed Oct. 1864.*

10 November 1912: *Directly north of this monument and considerably higher than it . . . is a sarcophagus the south side of which is cut with this inscription: Louisa Rodgers Meigs daughter of Commodore John Rodgers . . . wife of Gen. Montgomery C. Meigs. . .* [John Meigs' mother (1816–1878)].

II-11
Arlington, Va.
Tomb of Lieut. Meigs—made about 1900
[John Meigs was the son of Gen. Montgomery C. Meigs (1816–1892) who had a big role in the 1864 creation of the Arlington National Cemetery. The elder Meigs is famous for his engineering and architectural contributions to Washington, D.C.[2]]

II-12
Arlington, Confederate Marker and Plot 1908

II-13
Arlington, Confederate Markers, 1908

17 August 1912: *An old section of Arlington national cemetery, dedicated to the burial of colored soldiers of the Union before the opening of the new addition to Arlington, is seldom entered by tourists. . . . It may be reached in two ways: these are by the northeast gate or by following the steep gravel road that leads down from the rear of the mansion into the deep woods and ravines to the north. The east entrance leads between two tall urn-capped white columns inscribed with the names of two Federal generals Ord and Wetzel . . . about 2500 graves are here. One large plot is given over to the graves of 'contrabands,' runaway slaves who died under the protection of the Union forces around Washington.*

The field of graves lies between the Seneca sandstone north wall and a little stream on the south side that trickles down through the impressive woods, woodland yet untouched by the grave diggers spade. . .

II-14
Arlington Cemetery, (Colored)

II-15
Arlington, Sampson Tomb
[William Thomas Sampson (1840–1902) was a naval hero of the Spanish American War[3]]

II-16
Arlington, Monument of Midshipman Cruse, 1907

II-17

Arlington Graves, 1914

[A May 1905 "Where Sleep the Brave" article appeared featuring copies of Rambler glass negatives.]

II-18

Arlington—Maine Monument (First)

[The Battleship Maine was blown up in Havana Harbor in 1898. The mast was placed in Arl. Cemetery in 1913.]

8 December 1918: *The number of interments at Arlington on June 30, 1917 was 25,006 and of this number 4710 were 'unknown' being the remains of men gathered up from the civil war battles near Washington. Acres of graves are dug at Arlington each year and in 1920, when the work of bringing back the dead from France, wide fields . . . will be given over to new graves.*

II-19

Arlington—Making new graves by the Acre

[The Arlington Naval Radio Station towers, one 600 feet and two 450 feet, are dimly shown in the background. On a portion of Ft. Myer transferred to the Navy, these were erected by 1913.[4]]

II-20
Revolutionary Graves, Arlington 1907

II-21
Arlington—Amphitheatre Unfinished
[It was dedicated in May 1920.]

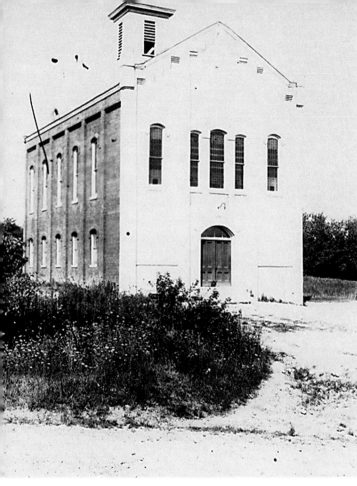

II-22
Church (colored) at Fort Albany, Arlington, Va. 1917

7 March 1915: *The Rambler followed the old north and south Post road which leads along the front of Arlington [Cemetery]. Walking southerly along the road from the Aqueduct and passing the southeast end of Arlington wall, a steep grade leads to the crossing of the electric railway which runs from Washington by way of the highway bridge* [14th Street Bridge area today] *and Arlington Junction* [to points south and west]. *Crossing the Columbia Pike and climbing the grade beyond Ft. Albany ruins* [he comes to] *Mt. Zion Colored Baptist Church. It is a bold brick structure with red sides, a dun front and was erected in 1884. The congregation was organized by ex-slaves. . . .* [Before that] *the congregation worshipped in a small frame building in the nearby settlement of Freedman's City.*

Below: II-23
Queen City (Colored) Arlington
[Queen City, established when the Freedman's Village was phased out in the late 1800s, lay along Columbia Pike east of Arlington Ridge Road—under the present day complex of roads around the Pentagon. A 26 January 1908 unsigned article refers to Queen City.]

II-24

Roach House on road to Alexandria
[A two-story, four-columned portico
later replaced the front entrance.]

Continuing south from the church [on Arlington Ridge Road which at that time continued from the eastern edge of the Cemetery toward Alexandria] . . . *on the crest of the ridge you see two tall square chimneys, heavy red brick walls, white pillared porches and bright green shutters. It is a noble old house . . . and you note that some new owner has taken it under his charge.*

Long before the Civil War that house was the home of James Roach, a considerable landholder thereabouts. He owned the grist mill on Four Mile Run. . . . As a contractor, he made much money out of the building of the Loudoun and Hampshire railroad. [No longer standing on South Arlington Ridge Road (it was razed on 21 November 1965[4a]), this house called "Prospect Hill" was built on these Virginia highlands overlooking Washington and Arlington by James Roach, circa 1841. The previously mentioned Fort Albany, one of the Civil War defenses of Washington, D.C., was built on part of the Roach farm.[5]]

II-25

Colored group near Fort Richardson 1915
[Fort Richardson was another of the Civil War Defenses of the Capital City. It was located west south-west from Fort Albany in the present day Army and Navy Country Club area.]

27

Left: II-26

Hume School

[The Hume School standing at 1801 South Arlington Ridge Road, now the headquarters of the Arlington Historical Society, was built in 1891 and named for Frank Hume (1843–1905), an educational and civic leader of Arlington County. Mr. Hume purchased 600 acres in 1879 on which he erected his home, "Warwick." It was burned in 1921.]

1 July 1917: *The house of the treasures which the Rambler described* [the Swann home, in an earlier article] *sits on a hill on the south side of Four Mile Run and just above the new automobile road leading from Arlington to Alexandria, and which crosses the tracks of the Alexandria electric railway at Hume. The splendid old home of Frank Hume with its familiar cedars and great oaks, is the next place to the house of relics. If you leave the Alexandria car at Hume station and walk along the road toward Washington for about 300 yards, you will see on the left 3 or 4 wooden steps that lift one up the bank by the roadside. From these steps a rugged path leads up the hill to the interesting house. There lives Mrs. Susan Calvert and her daughter.*

Same 1 July 1917 article: *On a hill above the Wash. Alex. Boulevard and overlooking Preston, is an old house bearing the name of Mount Auburn. It was the land of Thomas William Swann, the son of Charles Alexander Swann and whose wife was Helen Mary Chapman. It was built just as the Civil War closed. Their daughter whose maiden name was Susan Pearson Alexander Swann lives there today. She married George Edward Calvert of the Mount Airy Calverts of Maryland. With her lives her daughter, Miss Helen.*

II-27

Mrs. Susan Calvert and daughter at "Preston" [Mount Auburn]—*between Washington and Alexandria near Hume.* ["Mrs. Susan Pearson Alexander Calvert and Miss Helen Chapman Calvert" is the caption on the published photo.]

PRESTON

7 October 1917: *Preston was one of the large plantations near Washington. It was the name given to that tract of 6000 acres* [that was patented to Robert Howson in 1669 who sold to John Alexander a month later].

14 October 1917: *On the lands of Preston stand the city of Alexandria and all the villages between that place and Washington.*

7 October 1917: *Two other famous estates were carved out of Preston* [land, "Abingdon" and "Arlington"]. *The four houses of Preston, which succeeded one another nearly on the same site have passed away. A few bricks and weeds mark where the last house of Preston stood and near that spot is the burial ground where many of the people of Preston were buried.* [These burials were moved to Pohick Church.] *That part of Preston which the Rambler is immediately concerned lies along the Potomac river from the south shore of Four Mile Run to a point near the north line of Alexandria. Preston extended from the river westward into those high green hills which rise to the west of the steam and electric railway tracks leading between Washington and Alexandria. The great Potomac freight yards, the largest freight yards east of the Ohio River, have been built on the land of Preston.*

[Just north of the freight yards and Four Mile Run, also on the original Preston tract, stood Abingdon, the ruins designated by an historical marker which can be seen today on the hill above the National Airport between the two parking garages. There is a directional sign to the marker in the new terminal walkway. Abingdon was the plantation home of the descendants of the 1669 purchaser of the Howson patent (Preston), John Alexander. In 1778, John Parke Custis, Martha Washington's son, contracted with the then Alexander heir to purchase Abingdon.]

14 September 1912: *Steam shovels are eating their way into the birthplace of Nellie Custis* [born

II-28
Abingdon [National Airport Site], *Nellie Custis Birthplace*

1779], *granddaughter of Mrs. George Washington and ward and adopted daughter of George Washington. For years these shovels have been lifting trainloads of yellow clay out of the fields of Abingdon . . . and the clay is being molded and baked into bricks for the upbuilding of Washington city. Year after year the shovels have dug nearer to the weather-beaten frame house. . . . Now the deep clay pits are but a few yards from the house. A walk of half a mile from the stations Addison, Virginia Highlands, and Four Mile Run will bring one to this house. Part of the walk will be over dirt road, part over paths through fields and part along a footway through clay pits. The house is seen from the electric and steam lines. It is an ordinary frame farm house facing east and west, white painted but not freshly, with green shutters, a hip roof shingled, red brick chimneys at the north and south ends and a scattering grove of big trees in the front and sides. Most of the land between the traffic lines and the house has been cut down from 15 to 30 feet. Deep clay gulches extend in front and to the sides of the garden that surrounds the house.* [Abingdon was destroyed by fire 5 March 1930.]

II-29
Nellie Custis Birthplace, Abingdon, Va. 1908

II-30
*Nellie Custis Birthplace,
Abingdon, Va. 1908*

[The town of Alexandria was formally chartered in 1748 on Preston land owned by John Alexander for whom Alexandria was named. By the time of the Rambler's Alexandria photos, the port town was still viable though not the thriving seaport of yesteryear.]

II-31
Alexandria River Front, winter [probably taken in 1908, the date his published Alex. waterfront photo was made which appeared in his April 25, 1920 article.[6]]

II-32
Alexandria Water Front [from a slightly different angle.]

II-33

Alexandria Water Front, [Taken to the left of the previous photo.]

II-34

Alexandria Wharf Scene [Taken further left of the last photo. The following
appears on the building in the left background: "Grain Elevators, (Burr)oughs Sons & Co. . . .
Feed Mills" [probably T. F. Burroughs who was a merchant
in Alexandria in the late 1800s and early 1900s.[7]]

II-35

Water Front, Alexandria, Va., 1912

[This photo, showing the Strand between Prince and King Streets, was taken further to the left of the last one, but evidentally at a different time. There is snow on the roofs and the signs on the left building are missing.]

II-36

King Street and the Strand 1903

[This is the first block of King Street up from the Potomac River and the ferry building where passengers departed for and arrived from Washington City.

The Strand was a three block lane along the waterfront between Cameron and Duke Streets. The three buildings to the right were between the Strand and Union Streets. They appear in a photo on page 124 of Smith and Miller's *A Seaport Saga*,[8] in a view down King Street to the ferry building.]

II-37

Alexandria Streets 1912

[Beyond the three buildings in Photo No. 36 further up King Street, just west of Union Street, is the F. S. Harper Grocer building on the N.W. corner. "Harper, Frank S., 101–103 King" is listed in the 1906 Hill's *Virginia Business Directory and Gazetteer*, p. 161.]

II-38

Alexandria Street Scene 1909. [Union Street with its railroad tracks—looking south from King Street. The address of Walter Roberts whose sign appears on the side of the building along with "Sucrene Feeds" is listed in Hill's 1906 *Gazetteer* as 106 S. Union.]

II-39

Street Scene, Alexandria, Va., 1910

II-40

Alexandria, Va., Street Scene (town hall)

35

II-41
Alexandria—Sarten, John 1905

28 March 1915: *John Sarten again. It is always pleasant to welcome old friends and record their return. . . . Some of these negatives were made several years ago. One . . . was that of an old man in a high-peaked, rough-and-ready hat, and wearing on his shoulders a military cape of a cut and style that is not now the military vogue. His name is John Sarten. The Rambler met him on a street in Alexandria, made his acquaintance, and took his picture. . . . The mail a few days ago brought . . . the following letter:*

Dear Sir:

In looking over the Sunday Star of Jan. 24th, I was very much interested in an article . . . the quaint old man with the cape on happened to be my husband's grandfather, and from the way the article read I am aware you think he has passed away, and I am very glad to tell you he is still very much alive and is almost as active as he was when you took his picture in Alexandria.

He is still living on his farm near Franconia, Va., all alone, and I am writing this to you so that if you ever care to visit him in your rambles again you will know where to find him. He still remembers when you took his picture and also has the one you sent him.[8a]

II-42
Alexandria Cigar Store 1910, Joe's friend

Below: II-43
Alexandria Church 1915
[Presbyterian Meeting House, 321
South Fairfax Street.]

II-44

Alexandria, Va. Carlyle House 1907

[123 North Fairfax Street. To the far right, in front of the entrance to the Carlyle House, is the back of
the nineteenth century hotel that was built in front of the mansion. The hotel was torn down after the 1979
purchase by the Northern Virginia Regional Park Authority, which was responsible for the restoration of
John Carlyle's eighteenth century show place (General Braddock's headquarters in 1755).]

II-45

Alexandria Post Office 1915
[On the corner of South St. Asaph and
Prince Streets. Built in 1858, this Custom
House also housed the Post Office.[9]]

II-46

Lafayette House

[301 S. St. Asaph Street. It was built in 1815 by Thomas Lawrason whose widow loaned her house to Lafayette and his staff for a month in 1824.]

II-47

Alexandria-Lyceum

[201 South Washington Street. Built in 1839 and restored in 1974 for the first Bicentennial Center in Virginia.]

II-48

Alexandria—Old house 1915

[209 and 207 South Washington Street—both of these houses were destroyed by 1965.[10] The building to the right, somewhat hidden by a tree, is the Lyceum at 201.]

Left: II-49

Confederate Monument, Alexandria, Va.

[At the intersection of Washington and Prince Streets.]

40

II-50

*Confederate Monument,
Alexandria, Va. 1916*

II-51

Confederate Monument, Alexandria, Va. 1916

II-52

*Alexandria, Va. Street Scene near
Confederate Monument*

41

II-53

Horse and Buggy—Alexandria

Below: II-54

Alexandria—Cobble Stones on Washington Street, 1912

Above: II-55

The Lee House, Alexandria, Va. 1907
[The Lloyd House at 220 North Washington
Street was built in 1797 and purchased in 1969
by the City of Alexandria to be used
as an adjunct to the Alexandria Library.]

Right: II-56

Alexandria, Va. Christ Church
[An unsigned article concerning Christ Church
appeared in a 12 September 1909 *Star* edition.]

II-57
Alexandria, Children Group
Walcott, Harriet and others 1910

Below: II-58
Alexandria, Children Group
Palm Sunday.

II-59

Alexandria Cobblestone Breaking 1915., Hessian Pavement

[Cobblestones which had paved Alexandria streets were taken up in 1912–1913 and stored on this lot at Cameron and Henry Streets. The stone crusher to the left crushed the cobblestones into smaller bits to be used on roads.[11]]

II-60

Negro—Alexandria—"Used in Bull Run Story" 1906

II-61

Alexandria Group in Doorway, 1908

II-62
Alexandria
Herbert House,
Jefferson 1906
[More information may
be obtained in an
unsigned 26 April 1908
article in which Jefferson
Relics in Alexandria are
mentioned.]

II-63
Alexandria, Jefferson/Herbert children, 1906

II-64

Alexandria—Crittenden, Supt.
National Cemetery 1907
[The National Cemetery is located on Wilkes Street extended. In the Rambler's 24 May 1914 article he writes that:] *In the Alexandria National Cemetery on the wall of the superintendent's lodge is a bronze tablet which tells: 'Established in 1862; Interments 3,570: Known 3,467: Unknown 103.' It was the first national cemetery set aside for the graves of Civil War soldiers.*

II-65

Mr. Crittenden at National Cemetery
Alexandria, Va. 1906

II-66

Confederate Grave Markers

[The plaque reads:] "Under this mound lie the remains of thirty-four Confederate Soldiers which were disinterred from the Alexandria Soldiers Cemetery (Federal) and reinterred in this ground [at Christ Church Graveyard] on the 27th day of December 1879 under the auspices of the 'Southern Memorial Association' of Alexandria, Va. These men were prisoners of war who died in Federal Hospitals in this city."

II-67

Jones Point Lighthouse

[Located on the southeastern tip of Alexandria, the Jones Point Lighthouse was in operation 1856 thru 1919.[12] Unsigned articles 18 August and 21 September 1907 refer to the lighthouse.]

II-68

Jones Point Lighthouse, Alexandria, Va., 1907.
[At this place the first boundary stone of the District of Columbia was set. It is on the other side of the building in the embankment close to the river.]

II-69

Lighthouse Keeper, Jones Point, Alexandria, Va.

II-70

Group near Jones Point, Alexandria, Va., 1910

II-71

Alexandria Group—Children in Boat, Pickett 1920

II-72

Alexandria, Va., Children and arrow heads 1910

II-73

Roberts Mill near Alexandria

[In his 22 June 1913 article, Roberts Mill on Cameron Run is mentioned. The mill was in operation in 1916 according to his 30 January 1916 article.[13]]

Left: II-74

Girl at Roberts Mill, Alexandria, Va.

II-75

Mount Eagle, Bryan Fairfax House
near Alexandria 1917
[It was demolished in 1968.]
13 November 1927: *"Mt. Eagle [was] the home of*
Bryan Fairfax - one of the Fairfaxes of Belvoir
and an early rector of Christ Church, Alexandria. . . ."
[It was located on North Kings Highway at the east
end of Huntington Metro parking lot, just west of the
Montebello apartment complex.]

II-76
Ballenger Group, Mt. Pleasant, Va., 1917

13 November 1927: *The Rambler and his friends stopped in at Mt. Pleasant* [on a] *cold afternoon. . . . Mount Pleasant* [was] *the home of the Ballenger family, which owned the land Fort Lyon was built on. . . . Fort Lyon, situated on Ballenger Hill on the opposite side of Hunting Creek (or Cameron Run)* [was] *built during the Civil War and* [formed] *the south end on the Virginia side of the defenses of Washington and Alexandria. . . . The name of the farm has been Mount Pleasant for several generations. Before the Civil War the farm was bought by Peyton Ballenger, whose grandfather was a Virginia soldier in the* *Continental Army. Mount Pleasant was in possession of Peyton Ballenger when the Civil War came on and Fort Lyon and Fort Weed with long lines of infantry trenches were built on the farm. The Ballenger house was taken over by Union officers.* [Fort Lyon stood northwest of the Huntington Metrorail Station, and Fort Weed sat in the northeast corner of Fort Drive and Monticello Road.[14] Peyton's three sons fought for the Confederacy - two were killed in action. The third son, Robert Washington Ballenger, returned home to take over the ownership of "the old Ballenger House."]

54

II-77

Ballenger Group near Alexandria, 1917

Footnotes on Chapter II

1. C. B. Rose, Jr., *Arlington County, Virginia: A History*, Arlington Historical Society, 1976, p. 176.
2. James Edward Peters, *Arlington National Cemetery*, Woodbine House, 1986, pp. 152–153.
3. Ibid. pp. 199–201.
4. C. B. Rose, Jr., p. 162.
4a. Brought to our attention by Sara Collins, former Head Librarian, Virginia Room, Arlington Central Library.
5. Eleanor Lee Templeman, *Arlington Heritage*, Privately Printed 1959, p. 58.
6. Richardson, p. 11.
7. *Fairfax County in Virginia, Selections from Some Rare Sources*, Fairfax County Office of Comprehensive Planning 1974, pp. 32–34.
8. William Francis Smith and T. Michael Miller, *A Seaport Saga*, The Donning Co., 1989, p. 124.
8a. The 28 March 1915 letter re John Sarten was brought to our attention by Edith Moore Sprouse.
9. Smith and Miller, p. 89.
10. Ibid., p. 164.
11. Ibid., p. 120.
12. Ibid., p. 79.
13. Richardson Index, p. 245.
14. Raymond M. Sawyer, *Mount Eagle, Hunting Ridge and the Civil War Forts*, Unpublished manuscript 1997, p. 10.

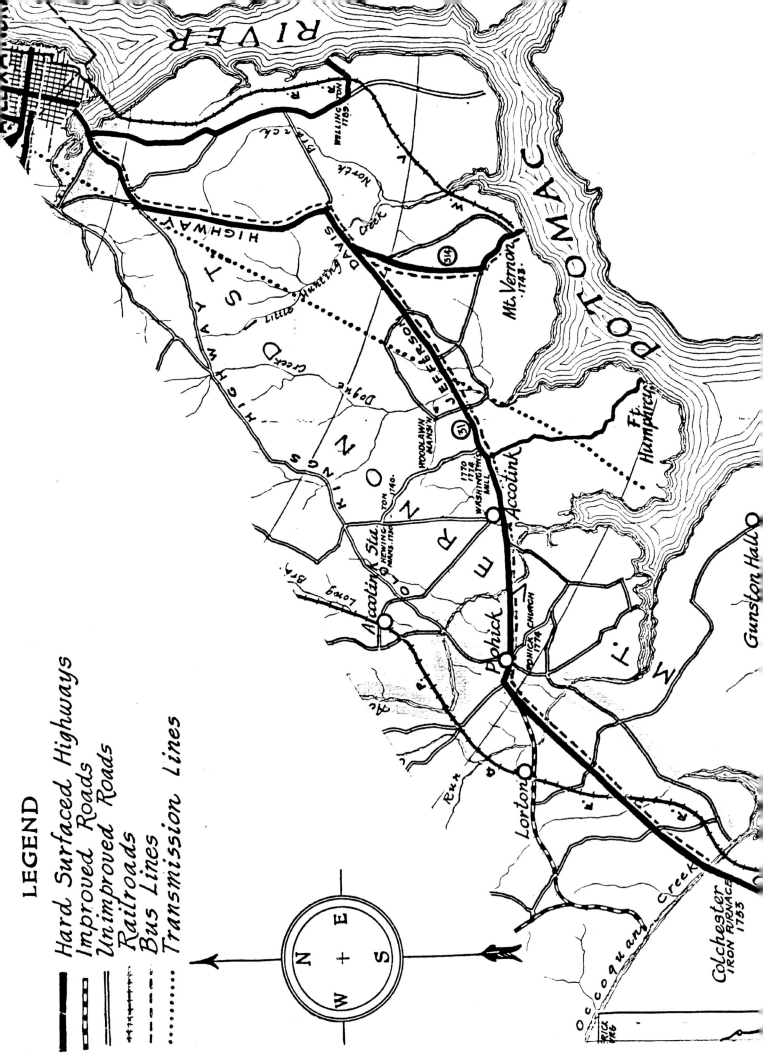

LEGEND

Hard Surfaced Highways
Improved Roads
Unimproved Roads
Railroads
Bus Lines
Transmission Lines

POTOMAC RIVER

Wellington 1765

North Creek

Little Hunting Creek

Dogue Creek

Pohick Creek

Long Brk

DAVIS HIGHWAY

KINGS HIGHWAY

JEFFERSON

Mt. Vernon 1743.

Ft. Humphreys

Woodlawn Mans'n

1770 1774 Washington's Mill

Hewing Mans. 1750.

Accotink Sta.

Accotink

Pohick

Pohick Church 1774

MT. VERNON

Lorton

Gunston Hall

Colchester Iron Furnace 1753

Occoquan Creek

N
E
S
W

Chapter III

Continuing Southward
to Fredericksburg

MOUNT VERNON LANDS

19 April 1914: *A traveller over the road between Alexandria and Mount Vernon may have pointed out to him a very old house that bears traces of former elegance. The approach to the house from the main way is through a lane lined with old cedars. The place is called Wellington, and it was a part of the Mount*

Left: III-1

"A Map of Fairfax County, Virginia." Published July 1927 by the Fairfax County Chamber of Commerce. Courtesy of D. Barton Betts

Vernon estate when the great Washington lived there. Wellington, before and after the death of Washington, was the home of Tobias Lear.

Tobias Lear [1762–1816] came to Mount Vernon as private tutor to the young Custis children, the grandchildren of Mrs. Washington and the wards of her second husband, George Washington. Lear from tutor came to be the private secretary of Washington, and at one time his military secretary.

III-1a
Roads near Wellington, Va.

III-1b
George Washington, Wellington Children, 1907

III-2
Wellington
Front View
1908

Right: III-3
Wellington, Group of Children

15 February 1914: *Gum Spring, Va., is on the road from Alexandria to Mount Vernon—the wagon road, not the electric—and was included in the limits of the old Mount Vernon plantation. It is rather an isolated place with certain historic associations. . . .*

Gum Spring is not an imposing settlement. There is a blacksmith shop, a colored church, and a few houses, mainly the dwellings of colored people, strung along the road at long intervals. . . . The settlement takes its name from a spring around which gum trees grow, or grew. . . . The Rambler was told on what he believes to be good authority, that today living around Gum Spring, *are a large number of colored people descended from the slaves of George Washington. Washington's body servant William or Will Lee lived at Gum Spring.* [George Washington's will specifies the following: "And to my mulatto man, Will, calling himself William Lee, I give immediate freedom."] *William elected to be free and settled on that part of the Mount Vernon estate called the Gum Spring tract. In 1802 on Mrs. Washington's death, many of the liberated Washington slaves also settled there grouping themselves around Washington's body servant.*

III-3a
Gum Spring Church, Mt. Vernon

III-4
Near Gum Spring, Mt. Vernon, 1908

Right: III-5
Gum Spring, Group at Well, 1905

[Mount Vernon, the home and plantation of the first president of the United States, descended to George Washington after the death of his half brother, Lawrence Washington, in 1752. He enlarged the dwelling in 1757–1759 for his marriage to Martha Custis, and again in 1773. By 1787, Mount Vernon appeared in its present form. [1]

The Mount Vernon Ladies' Association acquired the mansion on two hundred acres for $200,000 in 1858, and has preserved and maintained it through the ensuing years making it a national tourist attraction.]

Below: III-5a

Mt. Vernon, East View 1908
[Later views show the side porch and rail over the main porch have been removed.]

III-6

Mt. Vernon, West Entrance, 1904 ["Entrance to Mount Vernon which the Washingtons used" is the caption under a like photo in the Rambler's January 10, 1915 article. Earlier unsigned articles, 4 June 1905 and 15 February 1908 relate to Mount Vernon.]

Left: III-7
Mt. Vernon

III-8

Mt. Vernon, Mansion

Above: III-9

Mt. Vernon, April 7, '09, "Old Kitchen"

III-12

Mt. Vernon, Group in Woods
name forgot

III-13

Road near Mt. Vernon

Lower Left Page: III-10

Mt. Vernon, Mansion, 1915

[This appears to be the original Mt. Vernon Green House with Negro quarters in the wings. In a 1969 article written by Walter M. Macomber, the architect for the restoration of Mt. Vernon for nearly thirty years, he reveals that the present green house was constructed circa 1953 on the original foundations of this early green house—the same dimensions as drawn by George Washington.[2]]

65

III-14

Mt. Vernon, Site of Washington's Mill, 1905

[Unsigned 19 November 1905 article: *The site of the Washington mill is impressive. It stood on the side of Dogue creek and ships for Europe landed there. Today the creek where the mill stood is only navigable for skiffs. . . . Part of the foundation walls of the mill may be seen. The stable of a colored man, James Dent, covers part of the mill site and Dent and his wife . . . live in the miller's house on a little hill above the mill site. This house has been remodeled being two stories, whereas in Washington's time it was one story with a high hip roof. But the foundation and some of the framing of Dent's house is that of Washington's miller's house.]*

III-15

George Washington
House nearly on site of Miller's house on Dogue Creek 1904

21 March 1920: *One of the very early 'rambles'* *. . . was on the subject of Woodlawn Mansion, the great home which George Washington presented to his ward and adopted daughter, Nellie Custis, at the time of her marriage to Washington's nephew, Lawrence Lewis, in 1799. Loitering in the garden of Woodlawn, the mansion being at that time tenantless, he came upon an old gentleman who lived on a property adjoining Woodlawn, which is about two miles southwest of Mount Vernon mansion and on a ridge back from the* *old road that leads to Accotink village. The name of the man was Jacob Troth, one of the Quaker pioneers who came from Burlington County, N.J., in the 40s and bought a large acreage of the western lands of the Mount Vernon plantation, including the Woodlawn property, which they bought from Lorenzo Lewis, who had inherited the place from his parents Lawrence and Nellie Custis [Lewis]. The Rambler made a picture of Mr. Troth standing at the main doorway of Woodlawn.*

III-16
Nellie Custis, Woodlawn Mansion, and View From, 1904

III-17
*Woodlawn Mansion, Old
Friend* [Mr. Troth], *1904*

Right: III-18
*Colored Group,
Woodlawn Mansion, 1905*

III-18a

Lukens House near Mt. Vernon, 1915 ["Engleside"]

III-19

Mt. Vernon, Lukens family, 1910
[At "Engleside," the home of
Courtland Lukens (d. 1911). The *1906
Fairfax County, Va., Directory* lists the
following with Accotink addresses: C.
Lukens RFD 1 - Insurance (Sec. of
Fairfax Mutual Fire Ins. Co.), Louis
Lukens RFD 1 - farmer.]

III-20
Spring House, Lukens Place, Woodlawn Quakers, 1907
[Another view of the Spring House is captioned:
"Near Mt. Vernon on Quakers Farm."]

16 October 1921: *Two miles further* [S.E. from Accotink Station on the railroad] *Accotink creek comes to the ancient mill town of Accotink . . . . One mile more along its course it becomes Accotink bay which with Pohick bay forms Gunston Cove.*

III-21
Mt. Vernon, Lukens Cattle, 1910

III-22

Accotink, Street Scene, Quakers of Mt. Vernon [Sign on left building reads "Hotel" - the one on the middle building reads "Hotel Roby - Globe Beer."]

III-23

Quakers Mill on Accotink Creek, 1907
[Members of the Society of Friends (Quakers) from Penna. and N.J. settled in Accotink in 1846. It is believed that the mill stood at the site of the Eleanor Kennedy Shelter at 9155 Richmond Highway (Rt. 1), where Backlick Road joins Rt. 1.]

[On the peninsula between Accotink Bay and Dogue Creek to the east with the Potomac River to the south, stood the Belvoir plantation—now part of Fort Belvoir, the U.S. Army Reservation.]

10 January 1915: *Belvoir is about two and one-half miles south of Mount Vernon. By wagon road it is six miles from Mount Vernon. Much of this road is little traveled and twists through dense pineland to the bluffs that overlook the Potomac. The road winds for three miles through deep shadow. There is but one clearing along the way.*

Belvoir, in the colonial age, was one of the great estates of America. . . . [It] was the home of the first Fairfax to settle in Virginia - the honorable William Fairfax . . . who came to Virginia in 1731, settled on the Potomac, and between 1731 and 1736 built the house of Belvoir.

The mansion house of Belvoir was burned about 134 years ago. Forest trees grow where the house stood but one may walk upon the ruins and trace the foundation walls of the old pile. White oaks, black wal-nuts and beeches rise from mounds of broken brick. . . . In other parts of the wood are mounds of blackened brick marking the sites of smokehouse, coachhouse, sta-bles, distillery and other outbuildings.

Two hundred yards north of the main ruin, where the forest growth is heaviest . . . the wood is pit-ted with hollows. These are a number of graves. There is nothing to tell of the beings whose bodies were buried there. In one of these graves lies the bones of William Fairfax.

On the river shore to the north of the ruin is a brick building that was occupied by the Fairfaxes as an office. It is now occupied by a colored man, Robert Tait [Tate], and his family, and Tait maintains in the window of the house a lighted kerosene lamp for river naviga-tors to steer by at night.

III-24
Belvoir, Road to, 1904
[Under his published illustration in his 1915 article, he captions: "The Road to Belvoir where it passes through Washington lands."]

III-25
Mt. Vernon, Belvoir Woods
Site of Graveyard and House

III-26

Belvoir, Va., Tate's family, 1906–1907
[The caption under his 1915 published photo differs:
A mid-eighteen century building at Belvoir. His 7
May 1905 unsigned article, "Belvoir and Its Departed
Glory," informs us that: *On the river shore to the north
of the ruin are two brick buildings that were occupied
by the Fairfaxes of Belvoir. One of them is occupied
by a colored man and his family, Robert Tait, who
in the shadow of the larger house maintains a light
for river navigators to steer at night.
The smaller building is tenantless.*]

POHICK CHURCH

21 March 1915: *It is a walk of about six miles
from the electric cars at Mt. Vernon to Pohick Church
and the road will lead you around the enclosed lands of
Mt. Vernon, past the site of the Washington mill, by
Woodlawn, and to the village of Accotink. On the line of
the Richmond and Fredericksburg railroad, is a station
called Pohick at which accommodation trains stop and
a walk of about 3/4 of a mile from that place will bring
you to the church.*

*Construction of the new church building
[Pohick], which was of brick, with light sandstone trim-
ming . . . was begun in 1768.*

*Pohick church takes its name from a little water
course which ripples and struggles through the nearby
country.*

III-27

Pohick Church, 1905

Below: III-28
Pohick Church, 1905

Right: III-29
Pohick Church, 1905
Doorway and Sexton

Bottom Right: III-30
Pohick Church, 1905

III-32

Pohick Church, Children at Doorway, 1905

Right: III-33

Pohick Church, Rector - Pastor
Mellichamp (?), 1917
[The rector was Rev. Edward W. Mellichampe.
Figs. 31, 32, 33 were taken of and at the
south door.] *The doorway is the south one*
of Pohick Church five or six miles southwest
of Mount Vernon.

III-34
Pohick Church, 1905

III-35
Pohick Church, Tombstone Old, 1905
["To the memory of Mrs. Susanna Mills
wife of Mr. John Mills Merchant who
departed this life June the 12th 1774
Aged 39 years."]

III-36
Pohick Church, Scene from

III-37

Lewis Chapel, Gunston Neck
[In an unsigned 26 November 1905 article:
*Lewis Chapel is a Methodist church with a
small congregation. . . .*]

Left: III-38

*Pohick Church, Marker at Lewis Chapel, 1920
Site of the First Pohick Church, 1730–1774*
[26 November 1905: *Truro parish was carved out of
Dettingen parish in 1732, and a frame church was
erected at what is now Lewis Chapel. In 1765, the
church being out of repair, the question of a change
of site came before the Congregation and vestry.
Mason favored the retention of the site. Washington
won and the present Pohick Church was built and
consecrated about 1773.*]

12 September 1920: *Lewis Chapel, about a mile and a half southeast of Lorton, stands at the junction of the old King's highway between the Potomac and the Rappahannock and the road which leads from Lorton down Gunston Neck by way of Lebanon,* Springfield, Gunston Hall and Lexington to Hallowing Point. . . . *The chapel was abandoned as a place of worship fourteen years ago, when it was succeeded by a new building called Cranford Memorial, which stands up the road . . . about a couple of hundred yards.*

III-39

Gunston Neck, Ox Team, Luckett, 1905
[26 November 1905: *There is a well at this meeting place of the roads, and a rugged youth with his yoke of steers consented to pose for this photograph. His name is Arthur Luckett.*]

III-40

Pohick, Lewis Chapel, Group at, 1920

14 February 1915: *The Rambler has often walked from the railroad station, Lorton, to Gunston Hall, stopping at the site of the first Pohick Church and making side excursions to another Mason house called Lexington. He has then walked down to the delapidated wharf at Gunston landing, missed the boat and walking back to Lorton to miss the last train and then walked on to the cars at Mount Vernon—burdened with a camera, box of plates and other impediments.*

GUNSTON HALL
Gunston Neck

9 January 1921: [George Mason], *one of the prominent characters of the Constitution, lived at Gunston Hall on Mason Neck. . . . The house* [built by George Mason 'between 1755 and 1758'] *stands on land something more than 100 feet above the tides and about a mile back from the shore line of the 'cove'*

III-41
Gunston Hall, 1904

[Gunston Cove]. *It commands a broad prospect north and east, looking out across miles of water and including in view thousands of acres of field and wood on each side of the river.*

14 February 1915: *The Rambler knew Gunston Hall when it was almost ruinous. Several years after the Civil War, while it was in a state of great delapidation, it was acquired by Col. Edward Daniels who partially restored it.* [He added the cupola in 1875 to house his telescope.] *Col. Daniels came to Virginia from the north . . . and was an intimate friend of President Grant. From Col. Daniels, Gunston Hall passed to Joseph Specht of St. Louis who did much to rehabilitate the place. Mr. Specht died in 1902 or 1903 and Gunston remained in possession of his heirs for a few years. Then it was bought by Paul Kester who at one time owned Woodlawn.*

III-42a
Doorway, Gunston Hall, 1905

III-42
Gunston Hall, 1904

III-43

Gunston Hall, Box Walk, 1905
[Gunston Hall faces the Potomac River
in Figs. 41, 42, 42a, 43.]

Below: III-44

Gunston Hall, Rose Garden, 1905

III-46
Gunston Hall, Freeman's Wife, 1905

Right: III-47
Gunston Hall, Walnut Tree, 1905
[The published picture of this tree was labeled
"Jefferson Walnut Tree at Gunston Hall."]

14 February 1915: *Not far from the black walnut tree is a grave marked with a simple granite headstone inscribed, 'George Mason, Author of the Bill of
Rights and the First Constitution of Virginia
1725–1792.'*

[Figs. 41 thru 47 were evidently taken when Gunston Hall was in the possession of Mr. Specht's heirs. The following Figs. 48 and 49 show Gunston Hall back to its traditional colonial lines. It had been restored in 1915.]

III-48
Gunston Hall
[The Potomac River side.]

III-49
Gunston Hall, George Mason

15 August 1920: *Gunston neck [Mason Neck], water-bound on its northeast side by Pohick bay and Gunston cove, on its southwest side by Belmont bay and on the south by the Potomac, is six miles long measuring from the Kings Highway, or the present Accotink-Colchester road which crosses the 'neck' northeast and southwest from Pohick creek to Occoquan creek. The length of that road between the two creeks is 3 miles.*

Unsigned 26 November 1905: *A walk of a mile west from Gunston and through the woods brings one to the ruins of Lexington. The house must have been destroyed by fire not so many years ago.*

[Lexington estate fronting on Belmont Bay was built by George Mason of Gunston Hall for his eldest son. It was completed April 1775 when news arrived of the opening battle of the Revolutionary War in Lexington, Mass. The well, ruins of the foundation, ice house were in evidence in the 1970s.]

III-50
Lexington, Gunston Neck, Garden

III-51
Gunston Neck, Mason House
[A like photo printed in the 26 November 1905 article is captioned, "All that is left of Lexington." It is described as a little frame house near the ruins in which an old woman lives alone.]

III-52
Gunston Neck, Barn, Capt. Jim Wiley Parson Lee Massie's Place, 1920

III-53
Gunston Neck, Capt. Jim Wiley [second from left]
[Chas. Callahan center], *1920*

LORTON

8 August 1920: *Lorton is a little town 20 miles southwest from Washington and where the railroad and the auto road cross is a town of pretty homes set in blooming gardens with stores and a railroad station.*

12 September 1920: *Lorton is a Fairfax County place-name. It was the name of a store and post office, and a wide valley bordered by low ridges came to be called Lorton Valley. Through the valley flows Pohick creek . . . . When the railroad between Washington and*

Richmond was built across the valley in the early 1870s . . . a stop for accommodation trains was set down there. The stop was called Lorton.

The Rambler left the station of Lorton . . . and came opposite an old and 'homey' frame house off to the right. . . . On the broad, cool porch of the old house . . . were John and Mary Cranford Plaskett, he the first son of Joseph Plaskett.

86

III-54

Lorton, Va., Plaskett House, 1920

III-55

Lorton, Va., John Plaskett, [Son of Joseph, seated] and Wife and Some of the Family, 1920
[Joseph Plaskett (1813–1893), who opened the Lorton store and *was postmaster in one of the years follow-ing the Civil War* [when] *the Post Office Dept. named the office Lorton Valley,* was responsible for the name.
His place of birth was Cumberland, England, in a small town named Lorton.]

1 August 1920: *Colchester is on Occoquan creek and it was the first town established in Fairfax County. No town stands there now. . . . There is a railroad stop for accommodation trains on the Richmond and Fredericksburg line at that point and the name of the stop is Colchester.*

[Colchester] *was established as a town by an act of assembly in 1753–1754 on 25 acres of land.*

[The Rambler] *stopped at the old house in the picture of which accompanies this story. The stone foundation and the brick chimneys were in place when Colchester was a town, but its present frame part of the building is not so old. . . . It is now the home of John Weston, son of Lewis Weston. . . . Lewis Weston bought this property and rebuilt the house in 1850. Not far across the fields and closely sheltered by a thick growth of trees is a house which* [also] *dates back to the time Colchester was a town. It was the principal ordinary or tavern of the place and one of the famous taverns along that road from north to south*

III-56

Occoquan, Colchester Station

which was called the King's Highway. The name of this tavern was the Fairfax Arms. . . .

Through the front yard of the Weston home is a long depression about the width of an ordinary country road. A heavy sod of grass and clover covers it and you might not distinguish it from the rest of the green lawn. Yet before the grass covered it, that depression was a part of the historic King's Highway. In prolongation of the depression you will follow the trace of the old road down hill to the shore of Occoquan creek, perhaps 200 yards to the south.

Across the creek you can pick up the line of the long-abandoned road. From the south shore it climbs a steep hill and 2 centuries of traffic wore the road deep down between its banks. Then, since its abandonment, rains have washed it until along part of its course it is roughly gullied. Between the shore ends of the road ran a public ferry under the supervision of Ann Mason in 1736. And no doubt the Mason family, which then owned the land on both sides of the creek, operat-

III-57

Occoquan, John Weston's Home at Colchester

cutoff from Kings Highway north of Colchester to the mills upstream at the town of Occoquan diverted the north-south traffic.[3]]

III-58
Occoquan, King's Highway
Toward Colchester Ferry, 1920

ed a private ferry long before the Virginia legislature undertook to prescribe the rates of toll by making it a public ferry. At that point in 1798 Thomas Mason built a wooden toll bridge and that was a feature of the Occoquan region [until circa 1807]. *The road which this ferry and toll bridge linked up was the great north and south thoroughfare of the colonies and it was an important route of traveling during the youth of the republic.*

[The decline in the early 1800s of the town of Colchester close to the mouth of Occoquan Creek was due to the establishment of a competing ferry and then the erection of a competing bridge further upstream. A

III-59
Railroad near Occoquan, 1920

4 July 1920: *Nineteen and a half miles southwest from the White House as the crow is supposed to fly, . . . will bring you to a settlement that was once called Woodbridge but which is now called Occoquan and sometimes 'Occoquan station.' It was a station on the Richmond, Fredericksburg and Potomac railroad and the stopping place is about a third of a mile southwest of the creek.*

Up the creek, 1 3/4 miles from where the railroad crosses it is the ancient and historic village of Occoquan. There the tidal part of Occoquan creek, six miles from the Potomac, ends. Above the old village of Occoquan are falls in the creek and utilizing the difference in the level of the water, a flume or race which might be called a small canal was built ever so many years ago to carry water to turn the wheel of a cotton factory, now a gray and stately ruin [the cotton mill burned in 1862 at Occoquan] and also to turn the wheel of a venerable grist mill.

18 July 1920: *The village of Occoquan, the old mill town to which the Mary Washington [river steamboat] used to run on excursions . . . was established as a town by Act of Virginia legislature January 5, 1804, though it was quite a milling and manufacturing seat before the town was created.*

III-60

Occoquan Creek, Looking up under old R.R. Bridge [11 July 1920 published caption: Old Railway bridge, now a wagon Bridge, over Occoquan creek.]

III-60a

Old Occoquan Railroad Bridge

III-60b

New Railroad Bridge over creek, Occoquan, Va.

III-60c

Occoquan, Va., View over Creek, Below Bridge

III-61
Occoquan, View Down and Across From Railroad Bridge, 1920 [This looks like the location of the early ferry crossing.]

III-62
Janney's Mill at Occoquan Village

III-63

Occoquan, Large mill [Janney's]

III-64

Occoquan, Hotel and Street

FREESTONE POINT
Between Woodbridge and Dumfries

17 October and 24 October 1920: *The place of this 'ramble' is twenty-five miles below Washington. The direction is southwest . . . . It is one of those peninsulas or 'necks,' bounded by creeks and it juts into the Potomac river, forming one of the points that have become landmarks. . . . The upper boundary of this 'neck' is Neabsco creek and the lower is Powells creek. The tip of this neck which juts farthest into the Potomac is called Freestone point. It is at the upper side of the neck where Neabsco creek, merged with Occoquan bay, joins the Potomac.*

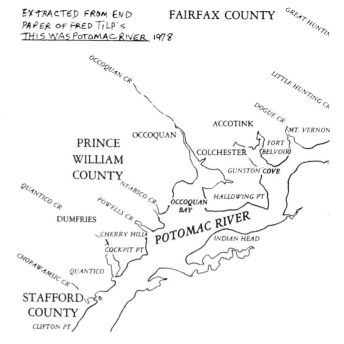

EXTRACTED FROM END PAPER OF FRED TILP'S THIS WAS POTOMAC RIVER 1978

FAIRFAX COUNTY

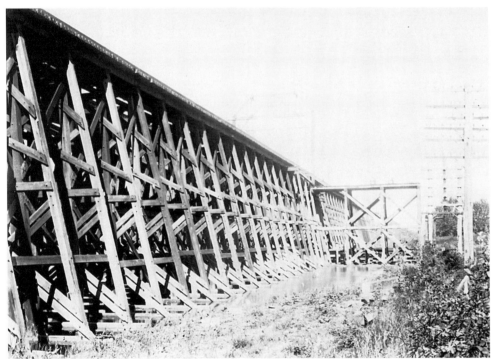

III-65
Bridge Neabsco Series, Powell Creek, 1920
[This bridge over the next creek to the south of Neabsco Creek (Powell's Creek) is probably similar to the "grim and grimy timber bridge."]

Below: III-66
Bridge over Powell's Creek, 1920

When the local train rushes at perhaps twenty miles an hour along the high and splendid 'fill' which was built across the lowlands, marshes and shoal water on the north side of Neabsco creek and roars across the grim and grimy timber bridge . . . it comes to Neabsco station, the railroad station [that] used to be called Freestone. Years ago the railroad crossed the creek a few hundred yards upstream or west from the present crossing.

. . . Following the trace of a road, the Rambler [first] *came to a mound of brick which had been a house perhaps half a century ago. Then, rounding a bend in the old road, he came in sight of the river and a ridge sloping toward the river. On that slope is a fire-ruin* [burned in 1910] *with two chimneys still intact. . . .* [This] *old house was the home of Col. J. W. Fairfax* [John Walter Fairfax, a Confederate soldier on the staff of Gen. Longstreet]. *. . . At a considerable distance from this ruin is a tall iron fence supported by stout granite pillars enclosing marble headstones . . .* [of the parents of Col. Fairfax, Henry (1774–1847) and Elizabeth Lindsay Fairfax]. *Their children . . . inherited the Freestone estate and lived in the house. . . .*

III-67
Freestone Point
Fairfax—Lee Farm Gate

III-69
Neabsco Creek,
Henry Fairfax Tomb, Leesylvania
("Henry Fairfax died October 6, 1847, 74th year of his age, son of Jonathan Fairfax and Sarah his wife, was born on the 29th of September 1774.")

III-68
Neabsco Creek
Fairfax Ruin on Freestone Point, 1920

[The Freestone estate was the site of the earlier Leesylvania Plantation which burned in the 1790s and may have been the brick ruins the Rambler first came upon. Henry Fairfax bought the Lee estate in 1825. This Leesylvania tract had come into the Lee family in 1675 but was not resided upon by a Lee family member until after 1747 when it was inherited by Henry Lee II.[4]]

RIPPON LODGE

III-70
Rippon Lodge, Neabsco [before 1921]

1 May 1921: *The house and lands called Rippon Lodge* [are situated] *between Marumsco and Neabsco creeks in Prince William County about 30 miles south and westerly from Washington. . . . It is a rare old place. The trail the Rambler took to reach the lofty ridge where Rippon Lodge stands led him through the lowland by the side of that wide creek called Neabsco. . . .*

[The house shown in Fig. 70, still standing today, was purchased and restored in 1924 by Judge Wade Hampton Ellis a collateral descendant of Richard Blackburn who had designed and built Rippon Lodge in 1725.[5] Blackburn's son, Col. Thomas Blackburn, was a contemporary and aide to General George Washington. Two Blackburns became mistresses of Mt. Vernon, Richard Blackburn's granddaughter and great grand-

96

III-71

Rippon Lodge, Neabsco

daughter. The first married Bushrod Washington in 1785, and the second wed John Augustine Washington. Both are buried in the Washington tomb at Mount Vernon.]

[Though not the house known today as Rippon Lodge, this building in Fig. 71 stood on the property. Could this have been the dwelling that was depicted in a 1796 sketch by Benjamin Latrobe as then being in the front lawn of Rippon Lodge?[6] The two-door entrance way might signify that it was built as a tavern with one door for the public entrance and the other for the privacy of the family. Perhaps it stood on the old north south Kings Highway (the Old Potomac Path) that in early times ran through the land of Rippon Lodge.]

III-71a

Rippon Lodge, Old Barn, Neabsco
[An iron barred window is shown in the basement of the barn at Rippon Lodge. "During the Revolution he (Thomas Blackburn) quartered a regiment of Continental troops on his place a whole winter . . . and had to imprison several for disorderly conduct."[7]]

III-71b

Smoketown, Prince William Co., Va. Group, 1921, See stories of Rippon Lodge. ["The hundreds of acres of thickly wooded lands located on the north shore of Neabsco, and owned by Washington lumber and firewood companies was called Smoketown because a cloud of smoke hung over the village caused by continuous burning of brush from intensive logging operations."[8]]

III-71c
Smoketown, Prince William Co., Va. Group, 1921

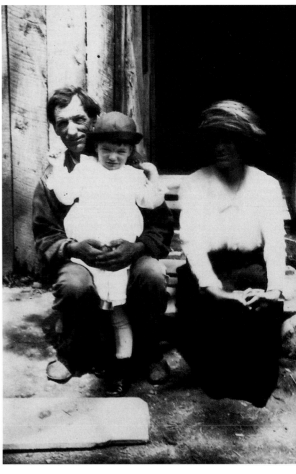

III-71d
Smoketown, Prince William Co., Va., 1921

98

DUMFRIES

6 June 1915: [Dumfries] *is on the old road from Washington to Fredericksburg in Prince William County and is on the upper side of Quantico creek, five miles above where that creek empties into the Potomac. For two miles above the mouth, Quantico creek is a stream of great beauty. In places it appears to be half a mile wide and only in a few places is narrower than two or three hundred yards, until about three miles inland from the Potomac, wide marshes border the creek and the stream becomes quite narrow* [due to years of silting]. . . . *Dumfries was a considerable city in its day, but the day as a city was long ago. The old Dumfries is now a ruin and a memory.*

Dumfries was settled by Scotch merchants and traders in the 17th century. [They] *settled on Quantico*

III-72
Dumfries, Quantico Creek

III-73
Dumfries House, 1906

99

creek near the head of navigation. The town grew with the country until it came to be classed with Williamsburg as one of the important places in the Colony of Virginia. It was a busy town before the cities of Georgetown, Alexandria and Fredericksburg came into existence. The settlement on Quantico creek ripened into an important town earlier than settlements on the Potomac at Rock creek and Hunting creek and on the upper part of Rappahannock river.

It was early in the 19th century that Dumfries began to decline. The creek was filling up in front of the wharves of the town, the size of seagoing ships was increasing, and other places along the Potomac . . . were reaching out for the trade of the region. About seventy five years ago, a great fire swept the place and destroyed very nearly all that time had left of the once prosperous town. . . . So it is that men today have their cornfields over the site of business blocks and in the fields you here and there catch the outline of a street.

[This old hotel in Fig. 73 and 74, Stage Coach Inn, was earlier known as Williams' Ordinary and Love's Tavern.[9] Built circa 1760 and still standing today on Main St. (Rt. 1 south), it is one of two buildings of architectural significance that survived the decay of the prosperous port of Dumfries.]

III-74

Dumfries, Girl in Doorway, 1906

[The fine stone doorway and the stone flat arches with fluted keys over the windows attest to the architectual quality of this old hotel at Dumfries.[10]]

[In the far right background of Fig. 75 is the other notable survivor of the early town of Dumfries. It, though, after much neglect, was destroyed in 1933 during a storm. This once elegant house, known as the Tebbs house, was built by Major Fouchee Tebbs. It, like the hotel, dated from circa 1760 and was similar in design and construction, both being large brick structures with cut-stone trim.[11] According to a street plan made of Dumfries in 1761, the Tebbs house faced the first street north of todays Route 1 south (Fairfax St.) and was located behind and to the left of the hotel, so that in Fig. 73 the hotel hides the Tebbs house.[12]]

III-75
Dumfries, VA, Man on Horseback, "Tebbs House" 1905

III-76

Dumfries, Va., Horses and Wagon, 1905
[The Tebbs house is back on the hill,
to the right. The wagon is on Main St.
(Rt. 1 South).]

Right: III-77

Dumfries, Anderson Cottage, 1906–1907

2 January 1916: *When the town of Dumfries on Quantico creek was abandoned as the county seat of Prince William and the center of the population of the county had moved fifteen miles to the west of that ancient and decaying city, the county court was removed to the highland and around it grew up Brentsville. That was in 1822. A court building and jail of brick were built, and both buildings stand useful to mankind today. . . . The old building at Dumfries, an impressive brick structure, passed through the fires which made most of Dumfries an ash heap and remained standing until long after the Civil War.*

When the county seat was removed from Brentsville to Manassas in 1893–1894, and the decline

III-78
*Brentsville, Va., Old Court House
now school, 1914*

III-79

Brentsville, Va., Old Jail, 1914

of the old court town set in, the court building became a school house, and it is serving that purpose today.

On the next lot to that on which the Schoolhouse stands . . . is a brick house, the residence of Dr. Bell and family. This building was the jail [Fig. 79 labeled by the Rambler as "Old Jail," looks more like stone or very coarsely laid brick]. . . . *A small number of the houses of early Brentsville remain and of those but two or three are in repair, the others being delapidated. The town was named in honor of Richard Brent, who was one of the early representatives and senators from Virginia.*

Footnotes on Chapter III

1. Thomas Tileston Waterman, *The Mansions of Virginia*, The University of North Carolina Press, 1945, p. 419.

2. Walter M. Macomber, *Mount Vernon's "Architect,"* Historical Society of Fairfax County, Va., Inc., Vol. 10, 1969, pp. 7–8.

3. Edith Sprouse, *Colchester, Colonial Port on The Potomac*, Fairfax County Office of Comprehensive Planning, 1975, p. 104, 105.

4. Eleanor Lee Templeman, *Virginia Homes of the Lees*, published by E. L. Templeman, 1985, p. 8.

5. Richard Blackburn Black, *Rippon Lodge*, Historical Society of Fairfax Co., Va., Inc., Vol. 9, 1964–1965, pp. 26–27.

6. R. Jackson Ratcliffe, *This Was Prince William*, Potomac Press, Leesburg, 1978, pp. 33–36.

7. Ibid. pp. 35–36.

8. Frederick Tilp, *This Was Potomac River*, Privately published, 1978, p. 321.

9. Ratcliffe, p. 49.

10. Waterman, *The Mansions of Virginia*, pp. 230–231.

11. Ibid. p. 230.

12. Ratcliffe, p. 54.

IV-1

Fredericksburg, Woman at Cemetery Gate
1st picture made in Fredericksburg, 1905 [Fredericksburg City Cemetery]

IV-2

Fredericksburg, Mary Washington Monument, 1910
[The 1894 monument to the mother of George Washington
replaced the original one erected in 1833.[1]]

Chapter IV

Traveling through Fredericksburg
Southeast to Montross

11 July 1920: *Under the date of August 1736, the Rambler came upon laws establishing public ferries 'on the River Occoquan in the County of Prince William,' and also to Nomini and Mattox creeks in Westmoreland county. In the same year of the establishment of these ferries 1736, the Virginia legislature authorized the creation of two Virginia towns which became famous. One was Fredericksburg and the other Falmouth. . . . Just before the passage of the ferry law the legislature chartered that 50 acres of land belonging to John Royston and Robert Buckner of Gloucester county, lying in Spotsylvania county, being part of a tract known as 'lease land,' should be laid off as a town which should be called Fredericksburg.*

IV-3

Fredericksburg, Mary Washington Home, 1907 [As a widow, Mary Ball Washington, the mother of George Washington, came to this house at 1200 Charles Street in 1772 from Ferry Farm south of Fredericksburg on the Rappahannock River. It was connected by a brick path to "Kenmore," the home of her daughter, Betty Washington Lewis.[2]]

IV-5

Fredericksburg, Group at St. Georges, Rectory
[St. George's Episcopal Church, built in 1849,
is located on the N.E. corner of the Princess
Anne and George Streets intersection.[3]]

IV-4

*Fredericksburg, Mary Washington House
Keeper of, 1910*

IV-4a

*Fredericksburg, Kenmore
House* [Kenmore was
built in the 1750s by
Fielding Lewis for his
bride, Betty Washington,
Geo. Washington's sister.]

IV-6
Fredericksburg, Va.
George Washington Lodge,
1921
[On the front of the Masonic
Lodge No. 4 at the N.E.
corner of Princess Anne
and Hanover Sts. is written
the following: "George
Washington (became?)
a Mason November 4th,
1752 in 'The Lodge at
Fredericksburg.'"]

IV-7
Fredericksburg, Va., Bedford's Hack, 1912
[On Caroline Street in front of Exchange Hotel.]

109

IV-8
Fredericksburg, Va., Street Scene, 1921
[Williams Street looking toward the Rappahannock River.]

Left: IV-9
Fredericksburg, Va.
Leader of Stonewall Band, 1921
Fredericksburg Story
[Andrew Benjamin Bowering posing in front of the Market House/Townhall, now Fredericksburg Area Museum/Cultural Center.]

IV-10
Fredericksburg, Monroe House, 1921
Fredericksburg Story
[Thought by some to have been the home of James Monroe between 1786–1789.]

IV-11
Fredericksburg, Va.
Old House
1907

IV-12
Fredericksburg, Va., Colored Group, 1910

IV-13
Fredericksburg, Va.
Prayer Rocks
Mary Washington
1907

IV-14

Fredericksburg, Va., Chatham - Lacy House, 1907

[Chatham was built circa 1770 by William Fitzhugh (1741–1809). It is located in Stafford County on the east bank of the Rappahannock River opposite Fredericksburg. By 1860, it was the home of the James Lacy family which was uprooted when Chatham became "a prominent landmark on the Union front line during the early phases of the December 1862 and May 1863 Battles of Fredericksburg."[4] During its occupation by the Union troops, Chatham served as headquarters and hospital. After the war, the ravaged brick dwelling was restored by the Lacys to the "Lacy House" the Rambler visited in 1907.]

IV-15

Fredericksburg, Va., Chatham, near;
Group of children, 1909

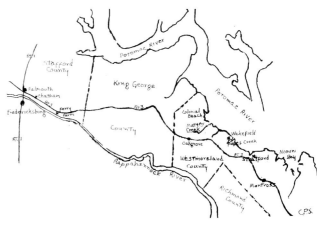

IV-15a

Sketch, Southeast of Fredericksburg. C.P.S.

22 February 1925: *There is one theory that when Geo. Washington's father and mother moved from Pope's Creek farm* [Wakefield] *to that on the Rappahannock* [Ferry Farm] *opposite Fredericksburg when George Washington was about three years old, it was because of the burning of the house on Pope's Creek farm. . . .*

IV-16
Fredericksburg, Va.
From the Washington "Ferry Farm," made 1905
[This photo was taken from George Washington's boyhood home, Ferry Farm, which is south of Chatham on the same side of the Rappahannock River across from the southern part of Fredericksburg seen in the background.
Note the steamboat.]

IV-17
Washington House on Ferry Farm, 1907
[A replacement of the original "Boyhood Home."]

IV-18
*Fredericksburg
Geo. Washington
Ferry Farm, 1906*
[To the far right is the
house in Fig. 17.]

IV-19
George Washington, Ferry Farm, Owner of Property, 1915

IV-20
Fredericksburg, Va.
Washington Farm,
Owner of place and my
livery man who shot himself

IV-21
Fredericksburg, Ferry Farm Group, 1909

IV-22

Horses and Buggies, Oak Grove, Va.

IV-23

Geo. Washington. Ox team at Oak Grove, Va., 1912

117

IV-24

Garnett House near Oak Grove, Va. in Washington Country, 1902

["Ingleside" was erected in 1834 as The Washington Academy of Westmoreland County becoming a private property in 1847. It is now the headquarters for Ingleside Plantation Nurseries, Inc.]

IV-24a

Wirtland Academy near Oak Grove
Westmoreland County

[The house was built in 1850 for Dr. William Wirt, Jr. After his death in 1898, Wirtland became a female academy, now a private residence and part of the Ingleside Plantation Nurseries, Inc.[5]]

IV-26
George Washington
George Washington [a descendant] *at Wirts Wharf*

IV-27

Mill – Washington

Mill on Mattox Creek [Wirts Mill], *1912*

9 February 1913: *Such a mill is standing and in operation on the old Washington lands in Westmoreland County. It is now called, and for a number of generations has been called, Wirts Mill because the Washingtons and the Wirts intermarried, and a large tract around the mill is called Wirtland. It is not far from Wirts Wharf, a frail, decrepid old landing place in Maddox* [Mattox] *Creek. It reaches out from the tree-lined, white and sandy shore to a point above the shallow shining water of the creek where steamboats may stop. After stepping off the land end of the wharf, turn to the right and follow a road that leads through tilled fields and also through thickets of pine and sweet gum. The old mill, its brick walls darkened and mellowed by age, stands in the upper part of Maddox* [sic] *Creek at the foot of a steep wooded hill. . . .* [The wharf and the mill were named by landowner William Wirt who was Attorney General of the U.S. from 1817 until 1829.[6]]

22 February 1925: *The Rambler's first trip through the Washington country in Westmoreland county was late in the fall of 1903 or 1904. He left the steamboat before dawn on a chilly day at Wirt's Wharf in Maddox* [Mattox] *Creek, walked to Laurel Grove farm, to the home of Lawrence Washington (Uncle Lal); on to Blenheim, then occupied by Mrs. Lena Washington Hungerford; then to Wakefield; was taken over the farm by John E. Wilson, the owner; had dinner with Mr. Wilson; walked to Potomac Mills, and got to the hotel at Montross about 10 at night. A walk of something like 25 miles with a heavy camera and two dozen plates. Tired? You bet.*

IV-28

Geo. Washington, Laurel Grove House, Group, 1904

Since then he has made many trips through much of that country, and during the time automobiles have come in, old roads have been rebuilt and new roads made.

From Wirt's wharf the road climbs a wide plateau. . . . About a mile and a half from the wharf you come to a farm house in a clump of trees with fig bushes and crape myrtle growing there. The farm is Laurel Grove and it is a Washington Wirt home. Mr. George Washington [descendant] *married Agnes Wirt, grand-daughter of William Wirt. . . .*

[The caption under the printed photo and the information in the Rambler's 1 March 1925 article identify those in Fig. 28: Nine year old Frances Wirt Washington and ten year old Elizabeth Wirt Washington in the front row, Mr. and Mrs. George Washington with George Lee Swanson Washington in his arms in the second row, and in the rear Miss Fannie Washington (married to Mr. Spillman) of Campbellton in that neighborhood. She is the daughter of Robert J. Washington and the "great, great, grand niece of the Father of the country."]

IV-28a
[Laurel Grove as
it appeared
in an unsigned 18
November 1906
article.]

121

IV-29
Geo. Washington
Mrs. George Washington
and Elizabeth, 1912

Left: IV-30
Geo. Washington
Elizabeth feeding ducks

IV-31
Geo. Washington
Mrs. Washington feeding chickens, 1910

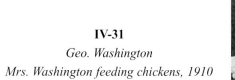

IV-32
Geo. Washington
Children of Agnes Wirt
Washington,
Laurel Grove
Westmoreland County, 1904

Left: IV-32a
Geo. Washington
Negro at Laurel Grove
Wakefield

1 March 1925: *The house at Laurel Grove burned and heaps of cinders lay for years among the warty locust trees. Mrs. Agnes Wirt Washington built a new house on the 'lower farm' at Church Point. . . . Elizabeth, now Mrs. Bowie, rebuilt Laurel Grove. . . .*

1 March 1925: *From Laurel Grove the Rambler followed the nearly level land for about a mile to the home of Lawrence Washington. Lawrence or "Uncle Lal," is now 89 years old but when the Rambler first came upon him he was only 69. Twenty years ago the Rambler wrote: 'A walk of a mile or so brings*

IV-32b

George Washington, Church Point, Va.
[Mrs. Wirt Washington's new home, 1912.]

one to the home of Lawrence Washington, a descendant of Augustine Washington of Wakefield, brother of George Washington.' [The names of Lawrence's children are Lloyd, Lawrence, Henry, Isabel, Sadie, Julia, Elsie.]

11 August 1918: *The house in which Lawrence Washington and his sons and daughters live today, though 4 miles from the site of the house in which Geo. Washington was born, is considerably nearer what is believed to be the site of the house erected on these lands by the*

IV-33
Geo. Washington
House of Lawrence Washington, 1915

Right: IV-34
Geo. Washington
Lawrence in barefeet, 1907
[With Mrs. Washington, Julia Washington, and Bessie Hungerford.]

IV-35

Geo. Washington, [Henry] *son of Lawrence*
Watering Horses, 1909

first Washington to settle in Virginia. Through the Washington lands flow two creeks - Popes creek and Bridges creek. They empty into the Potomac river about a mile and a half apart. George Washington in his life-time made many references to the Popes Creek farm and the house on Pope's creek [Wakefield]. [The Rambler reported the generally accepted theory that in 1652 the first Washington, John, bought a farm in this area locating his home on Bridges Creek westward from the Wakefield site on Popes Creek.]

8 March 1925: *A granite shaft stands on the site of the home in which George Washington was born and a small plot of land at the monument is enclosed by a tall strong iron picket fence. The monument was built by the United States in 1896, and then the Government bought two strips of land across the Washington farm to use as roads to the house site. The monument is on land that is perhaps 20 feet above tide and 100 yards from the steep bank of Pope's creek.*

Right: IV-36
Wakefield
Washington Monument, 1904

The Washington house stood back from the bank rimming much of the tidal part of the creek, and had an extensive view up, down and across the Potomac, there about 3 miles wide. The course of the steamboats is about 2 miles off the Virginia shore.

22 February 1925: *No fragment of the house in which Washington was born marks the site. No draw-ing of the house is known to have been made and most likely none ever was made. . . .*

It is believed that the name Wakefield was given to the farm on Pope's creek by William Augustine Washington, son of Augustine Washington, who was George Washington's oldest brother and who inherited the farm from Augustine Washington [their father].

IV-37
Geo. Washington
Frances Washington at Monument at Wakefield ["Washington's Birth-Place" is inscribed on the base]

IV-38
Geo. Washington
Graveyard at Wakefield

IV-38a
George Washington
Graveyard at Wakefield, 1906

[In an unsigned 25 November 1906 article, "The Star Man" wrote the following: "Wakefield is now one of the prosperous farms of the northern neck of Virginia. The owner is John E. Wilson, a Marylander. . . . The house he lives in was not a Washington home, but was built for Mr. Wilson. Great red oaks, tulip poplars, red cedars and long leaf pines that shade the house were started by him long, long ago. . . . This farm remained in the Washington family for a number of generations."]

IV-38b
George Washington
Wakefield House, 1904
[This Wakefield house was built in 1846 by John F. Wilson and in 1867 inherited by John E. Wilson who married Betty Washington, a direct descendant of George Washington's brother, Augustine. Their daughter married a Latane, beginning the ownership of the Latane family.[7]]

Below: IV-39
Geo. Washington
Wharf at Bridges Creek

8 March 1925: *Part of the farm has been bought by the Wakefield National Memorial Association, and this Association plans to buy the whole 'birthplace farm.' At the time the U.S. Government became interested in Washington's birthplace, it built a wharf where Bridges creek joins the Potomac. This was to make easier the way of visitors to the birthplace, the mouth of Bridges creek being nearer deep water in the Potomac than Pope's creek. The Government bought a strip of farmland from the wharf to the house site, fenced it with wire and called it a road.*

[In his 22 February 1925 article, the Rambler gives the theory
that Wakefield] *was burned while
the farm was in possession of William
Augustine Washington and that he
built a big brick house still standing
which he called Blenheim, 2 or 3 miles
from the Popes Creek house, because
of the loss of the older house.*

IV-41
Blenheim House, Wakefield, 1906

[Blenheim still stands in 1998, still owned and occupied by Washington family descendants. Present day information has the date of its erection for William Augustine Washington as 1781 after Wakefield's burning on Christmas Day, 1779.[8]]

30 May 1915: *Stratford, one of the Lee ancestral homes in Virginia, and the house in which Robert E. Lee was born Jan. 14, 1807, is in Westmoreland county . . . four miles by the usual road north of Montross, the county seat* [and about 12 miles south of George Washington's birthplace].

IV-42
Geo. Washington
Mrs. Hungerford and Children at Blenheim
[Mrs. Lena Washington Hungerford and her daughters, circa 1906.]

Below: IV-43
Stratford, Va.
Lee's Birthplace, 1912

IV-44
Stratford, Va.
Lee's Birthplace,
Outbuilding

Right: IV-45
Stratford Barn
[Printed version says
"Stable at Stratford
Hall."]

The Rambler ventures the conjecture that the present Stratford was built about 1745 but it was built in succession to an older Stratford Hall or Stratford House which was destroyed by fire.

Traveling the main road you come to a wire gate overgrown with honeysuckle, and passing through this gate you enter an extensive field, sandy and apparently not particularly fertile. A sandy road leads along one side of the field and about half a mile away you see above the treetops the chimneys of Stratford Hall. . . . At the north and south wings of the house a group of 4 brick chimneys reach high above the shingle roof and the four chimneys in each of these groups are connected at their tops by brick arches . . . . Between each four

chimneys and under the arches connecting them is a platform which rests on the ridge of the roof. Around each platform is a wooden railing somewhat decayed. From these roof lookouts you obtain a view over miles of country, which is mostly wooded, and over the river.

The garden clearing around the big house and the outbuildings is perhaps 3 acres in extent.

1 November 1914: *As the Rambler steamed into Nomini Creek (after a good nights sleep on the steamboat) he felt a strong wish that all his friends could be with him. At the entrance the shores are low, flat and white with plentiful patches of bright green vegetation. Nomini creek stretches and twists around inland for 10 miles.*

IV-46
Nomini Landing, 1910

IV-47
Nomini Wharf, 1914

Historic Nomini Hall does not stand today. Fire destroyed it in Nov. 1851 but a deep pit and mounds of brick mark its foundation and its ruin. The present Nomini Hall stands a few yards in front of the ruin. . . . [The original] *Nomini Hall is intimately associated with the life and times of King Carter of Virginia.* [It was built circa 1730 for Robert Carter, son of King Carter, and father of Robert (Councillor) Carter.]

IV-48

Ox Team near Nomini

MONTROSS

11 October 1914: *A few days ago the Rambler was sitting on the fence before one of the two village inns at Montross and he heard a discussion as to which of the counties of Virginia was the first to erect a monument to the memory of the Confederate dead of the county. The claim was that Westmoreland was the first to set up such a monument.*

Montross is a long and scattered village stretched out for a mile or more on a fine road which leads from Nomini Landing and other points on Nomini creek to Colonial Beach by way of Baynesville, Potomac Mills and Oak Grove. It is in the county to the

Right: IV-49

Montross, Va.
Confederate Monument, 1910

southeast of the Washington ancestral lands around Popes creek and Bridges creek . . . . Montross is also about 12 miles from the Wirt lands along Maddox [sic] creek. Stratford the ancestral home of the Virginia Lees is 5 miles north of Montross, and 8 or 10 miles south and east from Montross are the lands of Nomini Hall, the estate of Councillor Carter, grandson of King Carter of Lancaster.

The road is the main street of the village, but there is a side way, wide and short, which turns off the main way at the court building. On one side of this short way is the courthouse, a venerable brick building, painted and repainted yellow since the Rambler came to know it. . . . Behind it stands a little jail. . . . The court building is darkly buried in the shade of paper mulberry trees. . . . Opposite the courthouse is the Confederate monument.

IV-50
Montross
Westmoreland County, Va., Street Scene

Footnotes on Chapter IV

1. Noel G. Harrison, *Fredericksburg Civil War Sites,* Vol. Two, H. E. Howard, Inc., 1995, p. 218.
2. Emmie Ferguson Farrar and Emilee Hines, *Old Virginia Houses Along the Fall Line,* Hastings House, N.Y., 1971, p. 110.
3. N. G. Harrison, Vol. Two, p. 192.
4. Noel G. Harrison, *Fredericksburg Civil War Sites, Apr. 1861–Nov. 1862,* H. E. Howard, Inc., Lynchburg, 1995, p. 102–111.
5. Calder Loth, *The Virginia Landmarks Register,* University Press of Virginia, 1986, p. 481.
6. Frederick Tilp, *This Was Potomac River,* Privately printed 1978, p. 323.
7. *Farrar and Hines,* p. 82.
8. *The Virginia Landmarks Register,* 1986, p. 477.

IV-51

[The courthouse at Montross as it appeared in an unsigned 25 November 1906 *Star* article.]

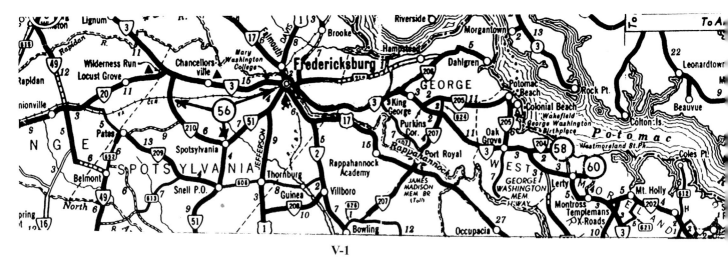

V-1

1940 Virginia Map. Courtesy of the Commonwealth of Virginia State Highway Commission.

Key to figure V-1 map

56. Fredericksburg-Spotsylvania Battlefield Park

58. George Washington Birthplace National Monument

60. Stratford Hall

V-1a

Road

Fredericksburg to Chancellorsville, 1909

Chapter V

Leaving from Fredericksburg
to Points West and Southward

10 May 1914: *The Rambler began his walk at Fredericksburg traveling over what was the Plank road, and which is still called by that name. It is a dirt road low, rough, rutty and hilly. The country is clay, yellow and red, and the road is extremely sticky in winter and early spring, and stiffling dusty when it dries out. The main travel over this road, as the Rambler observed it, is by . . . wagons that haul railroad ties which are cut in the Wilderness. Not a vestige of the war-time planking of this road may be seen on any part of its length. Before the war this road, because it was a great thoroughfare, was 'planked' with timbers two inches thick.*

On the first three days of May the Rambler was observing one of the greatest and bloodiest of American anniversaries—the anniversary of the battle of Chancellorsville or it might be more accurate to say the battles of Chancellorsville.

Following not long after the slaughter of Union troops at Fredericksburg, Chancellorsville cast a gloom over the north, heightened the hopes of the Confederacy, disheartened one splendid army, filled another splendid army with pride and exultation, wrecked the reputation of the Federal general commanding as a master of large strategy and a large body of troops, raised the fame of Lee and Jackson to the highest pitch and cost the Confederate armies the life of Stonewall. . . .It was, of course, a Confederate victory, but it was won at a big price. . . .

Out of Fredericksburg the road climbs a steep hill and crosses the uplands over which southern camps were spread in the winter of 1862–1863 and over which Sedgwick swept in his efforts to join Hooker at Chancellorsville. You follow this road for four miles then ascend a hill that leads up to Salem Church and you are then upon the field where Sedgwick, after close and hard fighting, gave up hope of reaching Hooker or taking Lee from the rear and moved off to recross the Rappahannock at one of the fords above Fredericksburg. Salem Church is standing and services are held there. It is a Baptist church. Breaches were made in the brick walls by artillery fire, but the breaches were later bricked up and you can see the patchwork. The older bricks that remain in the walls are in many places broken or pitted by fragments of shell, or grape, or musket balls.

It was not considered necessary to repair these injuries, and today the old walls have a pockmarked appearance as a result of the iron and leaden storm that raged there.

When the Rambler visited the spot a few years ago a fine granite monument had been erected at a point on the roadside about a hundred yards eastward of the church in honor of the 23d New Jersey Volunteers. . . . [It commemorates its services in the battle of Salem Church, May 3, 1863.]

. . . About a quarter of a mile east on Plank road from the . . . New Jersey monument lives a

V-2

Chancellorsville, Va.
Salem Church, October 1921

V-2a

Salem Church
Chancellorsville, Fredericksburg, 1906

138

V-2b
Salem Church, Va.
Salem Church, Sept. 1921

V-3a
Salem Church, made 1905
[Church yard with church showing faintly
in the left background.]

V-3
Salem Church
Window in Church, Oct. 1921

V-4
Chancellorsville, Va.
Monument, New Jersey Regiment – October 1921
[Another like photo taken in 1906 is labeled "Salem
Church Monument."]

Confederate soldier who was born on these fields. . . .
He marched with the Army of Northern Virginia from
early 1861 until 1864.

[In his 2 October 1921 article, the Rambler tells
of a small marker for the Battle of Salem Church, May
3, 1863, located on *what was the center of the
Confederate line and the place of the heaviest Union
attack.* The intensity of the battle at Salem Church is
described by a captain of the Ninth Alabama Infantry:
"so hotly was the ground contested that at one time during the fight. . . (Union troops) were at one end of the
church and ours were at the other. We had literally con-
verted the House of God into a charnel house. . . ."[1]

A description of the church as a hospital shortly after the gory battle is given by the Commander of
the 24th Georgia Infantry: "Here hundreds and

V-5
Chancellorsville, Va.
George Washington Lewis, Oct. 1921
Jackson Veteran

140

V-6

Chancellorsville, Va.
George Washington Lewis
Jackson Veteran

V-7

Salem Church, Marker

hundreds of the wounded of both armies were brought for surgical attention. . . . After the house [of worship] was filled, the spacious churchyard was literally covered with wounded and dying. . . .'"[2]

Today Salem Church, at the Rts. 3 and 639 intersection, is part of the Fredericksburg and Spotsylvania National Military Park.[3]]

10 May 1914: *It is about three miles* [from Salem Church] *before you reach Chancellorsville that the farms become scarce and that one enters the fringes of the Wilderness, the territory in which Chancellorsville lies. . . . Continuing on through the woods, one emerges into a broad clearing and in the distance gains the first view of Chancellorsville.* [Another description of the area in the same article follows:] *Chancellorsville is about two miles west of the eastern edge of the Wilderness, a vast district of heavily wooded country and containing great stretches of*

V-8
Salem Church, Va.
Old House, Oct. 1921

thicket and brake. Immediately around Chancellorsville there are several hundred acres of cleared land. In this big clearing the Plank road, the Orange turnpike and several smaller or less important roads converged. It was looked upon by the military strategists as a great position from which to conduct offensive operations against Lee, but also a most satisfactory place for fighting on the defensive.

10 May 1914: *When that section was swept with shot and shell, Chancellorsville consisted of one big house, with the usual outbuildings grouped behind it and at its sides. It was a big inn run by a man named Chancellor and it was patronized by travelers over the* [aforementioned roads] *that run from the Rappahannock fords and then off in the direction of Spotsylvania Court House.*

V-9
Team met On the Road In The Wilderness

V-10
Chancellorsville, Va.
Chancellorsville House, 1906

V-11
Chancellorsville, Va.
Man and Team, 1906

V-12
Chancellorsville, Va.
School House, Oct. 1921

Passing through Chancellorsville clearing, your road re-enters the woods and tangles of the Wilderness and, about a mile west of the Chancellor house on the right-hand side of the road, passes the spot where Jackson fell. A big, rough native boulder stands by the wayside and this was the only marker of the spot until the monument shown in the picture was erected.

10 May 1914: The shattered arm was amputated and Jackson was conveyed in an ambulance to Guinea station, a few miles to the south of Fredericksburg on the road to Richmond. As the Rambler remembers the distance, having walked it over rough and hilly roads, it is about fifteen or seventeen miles from the spot where Jackson received his wounds. Pneumonia developed and the Great Stonewall Jackson 'crossed over the river' and rested in the shade of the trees May 10.

Right: V-13
Jackson (Stonewall)
Monument where Shot
Wilderness near Chancellorsville, 1907

V-14
Jackson (Stonewall)
Guinea Station, 1907

V-15

Jackson, Guinea Station
Group, 1906

V-16

Guinea Station, Where T. J. Stonewall Jackson Died, Group

145

[No corresponding article was found to elaborate on these Rambler Spotsylvania Court House photos.

Situated on what was once the main road from Fredericksburg to Richmond, Spotsylvania became the seat of Spotsylvania County in 1830. It is described in the 1940 WPA *Virginia Guide* as "little but a green with courthouse, jail, and tavern."[4] Evidently it was also small in size when it was the site of a Civil War battle in May 1864. "In and around the tiny settlement," there were 18,000 Union casualties and 9,000 Confederates.[5]]

V-17
Spotsylvania Court House, Sept. 1921

V-18

*Spotsylvania, Va.
Sedgwick Monument
Sept. 1921*
[General John Sedgwick, Commander of
the Federal Sixth Corps, was killed 9
May 1864.]

V-19

Spotsylvania Court House, Spotswood Inn, Sept. 1921
[The description of the Spotsylvania tavern in the WPA *Virginia Guide* fits the Rambler's photo of the Spotswood Inn:
". . . Opposite the courthouse green, is a long rambling brick building with a roof that slopes forward to shelter
a veranda with heavy columns. The southern half, built shortly after the Revolution, was added to in 1830.
Though the building has been used continuously as an inn under various names, it has at time sheltered a school,
a post office, and Confederate military leaders."[6]]

V-20
Spotsylvania Court House, Jail in, 1921

V-21
Spotsylvania Court House
Jail, Sept. 1921

148

V-22

Spotsylvania Court House, Christian Church
Front View, Sept. 1921

V-22a

Spotsylvania Court House
Street scene, Sept. 1921

5 April 1914: *There were two places called Appomattox in 1865. One was Appomattox Court House and the other was Appomattox station, a stopping point for trains on the line of railway between Fredericksburg and Lynchburg. . . .*

Appomattox Court House, around which the Army of Northern Virginia and the Army of the Potomac *lay, where there had been some fighting and what appeared to be the final battle between these armies impended, was three miles to the north of the railroad station of Appomattox . . . . When the court building burned, the county seat was removed to the railroad, and there today is a thriving village which bears the historic name Appomattox.*

V-23
Appomattox Village, 1905

V-24

Bank of Appomattox

["The Bank of Appomattox building is still on Main Street but no longer used as a bank," as quoted from a 1996 note from the Mayor of the town.]

5 April 1914: *The* [first] *village of Appomattox, the place of Lee's surrender forty-nine years ago April 9* [1865], *has fallen into ruin and has nearly disappeared. Three and four houses have survived fire, storm, and neglect, but even these are warped and sagging, and the promise is that they, too, will soon rot and that weeds, followed by pine, will overrun their site. Two of these houses had long been abandoned when the Rambler passed that way. One was occupied by the large family of a small farmer, a stranger to that part of Virginia, who was unfamiliar with and indifferent to the great memories that cluster around that tragic ground. The other had been the Appomattox Hotel and is now the home of the overseer of about 1500 acres of the surrender ground, owned by Col. George A. Arines of Washington.*

V-25

Appomattox Hotel, 1908

V-26

Appomattox, House in, 1907

V-27

Appomattox, House on road

5 April 1914: *This hamlet at the time of the surrender was the seat of Appomattox County, Virginia. It was even then, after four years of war, a seedy and ramshackle cluster of nearly dilapidated houses. There was a group of dwellings, mostly of wood, a hiring stable, a hotel or tavern, a smithy, and a store or two that leaned around the sleepy courthouse square. The court building, which had stood there unnumbered years, burned down about 20 years ago and today the desolate square is cumbered with ashes, charred plaster, shattered brick. . . .*

You can walk through the garden of the house in which the formal surrender took place. That was the house of Wilmer McLean. It was a broad-fronted brick house, with covered porch in front and the entrance in the middle with a hallway through the center of the building from front to back. . . . Wilmer McLean, who was a man of peace, was living outside of Manassas to the northeast of the railroad junction . . . that is, in the

direction of Bull Run. . . . He wanted to get far away from the sound and the scenes of battle. . . . [He] moved to the county seat of Appomattox county, down in the neighborhood of Lynchburg and Farmville.

About 1892 the McLean house was torn down with the idea that it would be restored and rebuilt at the Columbian exposition at Chicago, but the plan did not pan out, it being carried no further than the demolition of the house. For years the piles of brick and lumber that had been the house lay rotting in the garden. That was the condition of the place when the Rambler visited it. [This house and the most important lost buildings have been rebuilt or restored.[7]]

V-28
Appomattox
Lumber of McLean House

V-29
Appomattox, Va.
Horse and Buggy, 1905

V-30
Appomattox, Va.
Hotel Keeper's Child, 1907

V-31
Appomattox
Log cabin, 1912

YORKTOWN

[Again, no Rambler article was located that expanded on his photos of historic Yorktown, the seat of York County at the mouth of York River, and where the American Revolution was brought to its close. On 19 October 1781, the surrender of Lord Cornwallis of the British forces to George Washington brought the end of colonization for the American people.]

156

V-34

Yorktown, Va., April 1921, Old House, National Bank
[As a photo on page 498 in *The Virginia Landmarks Register* shows,
this is the early eighteenth-century Pate House.]

V-35
*Yorktown, Va.
April 1921, Shield House*
[The early eighteenth
century Sessions-Shield
house was built by
Thomas Sessions.]

V-36

The Nelson House
Yorktown, Va., April 1921
[The Nelson house was built
by William Nelson in
1740–1741. He was the
father of Thomas Nelson
who signed the Declaration
of Independence and was
Governor of Virginia.
Cornwallis occupied the
mansion during the siege
of 1781.[9]]

V-37
Yorktown, Va.
Street Scene
April 1921

V-38

Yorktown, Va.
A group of Citizens
April 1921

Right: V-39

Yorktown, Va.
April 21, Yorktown Monument
[The Yorktown Monument, erected 1881–1884, is an
elaborate white marble column with the figure of
Liberty on the top with outstretched arms.]

Footnotes on Chapter V

1. Noel G. Harrison, *Chancellorsville Battlefield
   Sites*, H. E. Howard, Inc., 1990, p. 161.
2. Ibid., p. 162.
3. Ibid.
4. Work Projects Administration (WPA), Virginia,
   A Guide to The Old Dominion, Oxford
   University Press, N.Y., 1940, p. 506.
5. *The Virginia Landmarks Register*, p. 435.
6. WPA, p. 506.
7. *The Virginia Landmarks Register*, p. 34.
8. WPA, p. 461.
9. Ibid.

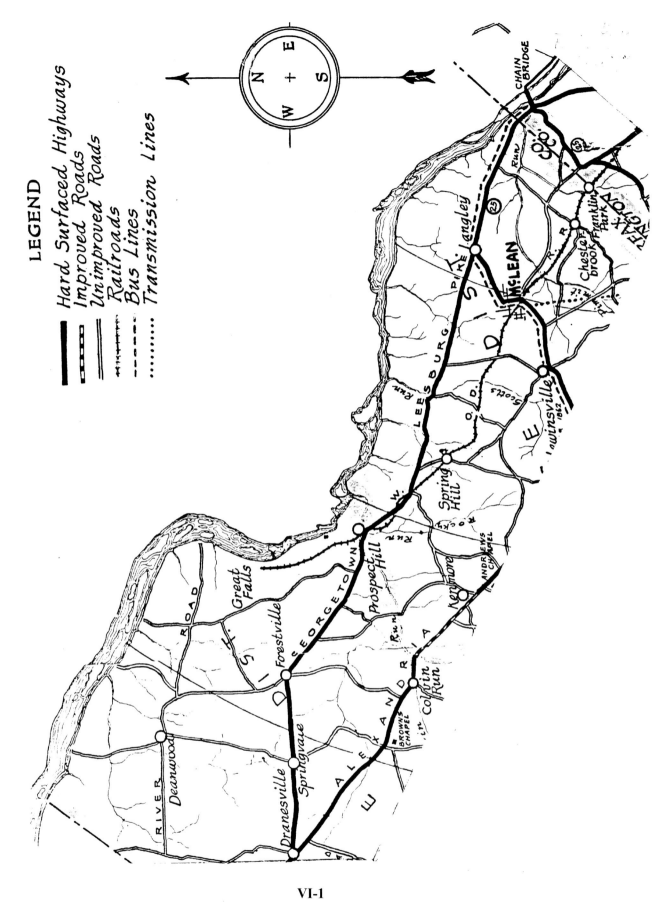

VI-1

"A Map of Fairfax County, Virginia" published July 1927 by the Fairfax County Chamber of Commerce.
Courtesy of D. Barton Betts.

PART 2. UP THE RIVER

Chapter VI

Rambling Northwesterly
from Chain Bridge

20 October 1918: *From the budding days of spring until the late summer flowers were in bloom and the greenery of the trees began to take on a sere and dusty look, the Rambler carried his readers through that country traversed by the Georgetown and Leesburg* [Rt. 193] *and the Alexandria and Leesburg* [Rt. 7] *turnpikes and scores of the old roads connecting those venerable and historic highways or branching off from them in many directions. He obeyed the call of each of these old roads whenever he thought it might lead him to an historic Virginia homestead, a ruined mill, a gray age-worn church or any other object of sufficient interest to form the subject of a story. A countless, or at least an uncounted, number of trails were followed through woods and fields.*

Naturally, that wide section of country divided itself into the valleys of streams or runs, as streams which are more than branches and less than rivers are generally called in this region. The Sunday trips carried him up, down and across Scott's run, Prospect run, Snake Den run, Wolf Trap run, Colvin run, Sugarland run, Cabin branch and through the village of Langley, Lewinsville, McLean, Tysons Crossroads, Ash Grove, Kenmore, Forestville, Surlingvale, Dranesville, Daysville, Sterling, and of course, that important village which approaches the size of a small city, Herndon. [No Herndon photos found in collection.]

2 August 1914: *If you cross the Chain Bridge which is an iron-truss bridge on stone piers, but which preserves the name of a four chain suspension bridge, which, about twenty years before the Civil War, was constructed at Little Falls in place of several earlier wooden bridges which had been washed away, you arrive at a gorge in the Potomac palisades through which Pimmit Run enters the river. A few rods beyond the Virginia end of the bridge you are confronted by a parting of the road. One way turns to the left* [Glebe Road], *crosses the rocky course and rushing waters of Pimmit Run and . . . climbs to the highland and emerges on an extensive and cleared plateau at the ruins of Fort Ethan Allen . . . an important link in the cordon of Washington's Civil War fortifications. . . . At this parting of the ways a shadowy road points directly ahead* [Chain Bridge Road], *high hills rising on the right and the deep and beautiful gorge of Pimmit Run on the left. This road also climbs a long steep grade and comes upon the highlands at the ruins of Fort Marcy, another of the Chain Bridge defenses. The road which you have followed since leaving the bridge* [Chain] *is part of the Leesburg and Georgetown Pike, which, after a good many miles of rough going, joins the Leesburg and Alexandria Turnpike at Dranesville, something like fifteen miles this side of Leesburg.*

VI-1a
Chain Bridge

VI-2
Pimmit Run, Chain Bridge, 1915
[Bridge across Pimmit Run]

14 January 1917: *After following the road from Chain Bridge up the steeps to where Fort Marcy stood . . . You will soon come upon a tollgate, and, though it is a new tollgate, it is not a new institution on this ancient way. . . . Beyond the tollgate—that is to the west of it— you will come upon a stretch of road where big cedars are growing in a straight line on the right and fine old maples on the left.*

22 February 1920: *On the right of the road west of the fort ruins is an old frame house which was the home of the Waggaman family. The head of the family in that house, which was standing before the Civil War, was John Waggaman. . . .* [According to the Rambler, John H. Soloman was the owner of the property in 1920.]

VI-3
Waggaman House, near Chain Bridge, 1915
9 August 1914: *The Waggaman home [is] now about one-half the size it was before the war and while the Waggaman family lived there.*

VI-4
Old Barn on Waggaman Place Chain Bridge, Va., 1914
[The Rambler thought this barn was used for stock brought by drovers on their way to Georgetown markets.]

4 February 1917: *Half a mile west of Fort Marcy ruins . . . stands a long-abandoned and weather-riven blacksmith shop which on more than one occasion the Rambler has used as a resting point. . . . It was the Faulkner Blacksmith shop. . . . The great highway from the Chain Bridge to the Blue Ridge leads by the front of the shop while at the west side is a dirt road which strikes off crookedly to the southwest* [Kirby Road] *and leads to Chesterbrook a mile and a half away. . . . One's course is level . . . for a couple of hundred yards or so. Then the road begins a steep descent* ["Slades hill was on that road," 9 August 1914]. . . . *At the foot of the hill you come to a branch, and a bridge. The branch is big Pimmit run, and close by this point another stream joins that which rushes beneath the bridge. That stream is Little Pimmit run. Here is an old mill site. Every vestige of this mill has vanished . . .* [except a] *trace of the mill race. Here stood Nelsons mill* [where] *the State Department records, hurriedly removed from Washington on the approach of the British from the direction of Bladensburg on that fateful afternoon of August 25, 1814, were secreted. . . .* [Where the government archives were temporarily stored when the British burned Washington City.] *That at least is the story . . . and was accepted when the oldest man who reads these lines was a boy.*

4 February 1917: *From the mill site the road leads across low wet land with Little Pimmit run on the left. . . . Soon the road climbs a hill and a few paces brings a small cluster of tombstones and an old frame house* [into view]. *That was the home of William Nelson, the miller, one of the big landed proprietors of the region of Washington. His grandson occupies the place today. . . . The great tract dwindled to a small farm.*

VI-5
Road near Nelson Place, 1917
[Published version is: "Muddy Road From Langley to Chesterbrook," Kirby Road]

Right: VI-6
Nelson House near Chesterbrook, Va., 1917

[Back on the Georgetown Leesburg Turnpike west of the Waggaman home and the Faulkner Blacksmith Shop] 22 February 1920: *Further on is the old house of Rokeby, the home of Basil Gantt during the Civil War and the home of his descendants today* [John Gantt and family]. 4 February 1917: *Nearby a rough lane strikes off to the right* [of the pike] *and leads north. It passes a group of farm outbuildings and then forks to the right and left. The left leads away through the fields*

. . . the right to a frame house. This is the Gantt farm [Rokeby]. *It is the remaining parcel of what was, a century and less ago, one of the large estates of Virginia.*

[It is generally believed today that Mrs. James Madison, on 24 August 1814, spent her first night at Rokeby on her flight from the White House before its capture by the British in the War of 1812.[1]]

VI-7
Gantt House, Rokeby, Leesburg Pike
[Georgetown-Leesburg Pike, Chain Bridge Road today
at this point]

VI-8

Gantt House, Rokeby, 1916, The Older Part of Rokeby

22 February 1920: *Still further west on the pike, a lane which leads to a highly improved road, strikes off to the right. It is the lane which leads to the Leiter place on the river, a house which because of the size and splendor is one of the famous mansions in the environs of Washington.* [It was built 1911–1912 by Joseph Leiter on ground that became the Bureau of Public Roads and the C.I.A. Headquarters area.]

VI-8a

[Leiter House in decline—not a Rambler photo—taken in 1942, ten years after the death of Joseph Leiter.]

Beyond that and before you come to Langley, another lane strikes off toward the river. . . . It is the lane [to] the old hall of Harmony Valley [which] burned about ten years ago and a modern house stands on the site, and here dwells James L. Reid, grandson of the founder of Harmony Valley

7 January 1917: [Langley] *is about two and a half miles from the Virginia end of Chain bridge and not quite a mile and a half south of the Potomac river. Langley is a hamlet of a schoolhouse, a church and several dwellings and set upon the north and south sides of the Georgetown and Leesburg road. . . .*

28 January 1917: *The foundation of the beginning of the hamlet was a tavern . . . which sprang up along those ancient arteries of trade and travel, the turnpike. The first of these was an old one in 1839. . . .*

It was the last stop the droves and drovers made on the road to Georgetown. The first of these taverns stood on the north side of the pike, close to the site of the present Methodist church. This tavern building was torn down about two years ago. . . .

[Across the pike on the southeast angle of the fork formed by the joining of Old Chain Bridge Road and Route 193, a second tavern was built in 1856 as a Drovers' Rest by George F. M. Walters whose home-place was Hickory Hill (now the home of Mrs. Robert Kennedy), the then adjoining estate south on Old Chain Bridge Road.[2] Today the tavern, *a picket post throughout the [Civil] war [and] at one time the headquarters of Gen. McCall,* is a private home at 1101 Chain Bridge Road.[3]]

VI-9
Langley, Va., Inn and Military Headquarters

167

28 January 1917: *So important a place did this little hamlet [Langley] on the pike become that a third tavern was opened on the north side of the road, east of the first tavern. . . . Halfway between the [taverns] was* the ancient tollgate. The tollhouse is standing now, being included in a larger structure in which Braden Hummer keeps a little country store.

VI-10
Langley Village Scene, 1918, [The building to the left is the Hummer store at 6324 Georgetown Pike.]

28 January 1917: *This brings to the Rambler's mind the little M. E. Church. It was built on the north side of the pike where the road turns off to Lewinsville, Vienna, etc., about the year 1859. Of course it was used as a hospital during the Civil War. . . . The church building today, remodeled and much improved, is the house of Douglas Mackall, the Washington lawyer. The building was hauled a few yards away and on higher ground.* The Methodists erected a new building on the site of the old. [The church building, now the Langley Hill Meeting House at 6410 Georgetown Pike, was built in 1893.]

7 January 1917: *About a quarter of a mile west from the schoolhouse and church at Langley, on the north side of Leesburg road [Rt. 193] and on higher land than that historic thoroughfare, is a large frame*

VI-11
Langley, [Douglas] Mackall House, 1918
[Now the Country Day School at 6418 Georgetown Pike.]

VI-11a
Langley House

house embowered in oaks, cedars, and pines. . . . It is a charming old house which has kept its youthful brightness. . . . This is the mansion house of the tract of land called Langley, and the hamlet of Langley takes its name from that tract. [The 540 acre tract "commonly called Langley" was bought by the Mackall family in 1838. The mansion house was destroyed by fire in 1934. Its site was sold and rebuilt upon.[4]]

22 April 1917: [The Georgetown and Leesburg road, Rt. 193] *roughens soon after passing the fine home and pleasant grounds of Miss Frances Mackall. . . .* [Douglas Mackall's sister who was then living in Langley House the home of their father, Gen. William Whann Mackall (1817–1891) and grandfather, Benjamin Mackall (1790–1880).] *It is a short walk, perhaps half a mile, to a point where a lane* [on the west side] *leads to a group of white buildings on a hill. At the foot of the hill by the side of the lane is a bluestone springhouse* [of great age]. . . . *The lane bordered by elms and maples leads up the hill to a big house where*

VI-12
Sharon, Va., Commodore Catesby ap Jones Springhouse, On Georgetown-Leesburg Pike, West of Langley

VI-13
Sharon, 1918

VI-14
Sharon
Commodore Catesby ap Jones, Leesburg Pike [Rt. 193]

rock walls were overlaid with plaster. The name of this place is Sharon and for nearly half a century it was the home of a distinguished officer of the old navy, Commodore Thomas ap Catesby Jones [1790–1858].

8 November 1914: *Behind* [the big house on the hill] *is another house in the same style of architecture and construction, but with a section of the front wall fallen out. Nearby are a meathouse, a smokehouse, an icehouse and a stone structure that was a bathhouse into which water was pumped. . . . Occupying quite an area are barns and stables . . . .*

8 November 1914: *The pike [Rt. 193] does not become depraved immediately west of Langley, but is travelable about as far as the hills that drop into and climb out of the valley through which Scotts run flows.*

28 April 1918: *The valley which the pike crosses five miles west of Chain Bridge is one that has been worn by Scotts run. . . . The rock-paved way of the Georgetown and Leesburg pike became so bad that traffic turned aside and took to the clay, first on one side of the rock bedded roadway and then on the other. The result of the side-stepping was to wear roads in many places ten feet below the grade of the stony pike.*

VI-15
Leesburg Pike [Rt. 193]
Scotts Run, 1915

172

VI-16
Road (Summer)
Leesburg Pike [Rt. 193]
near Prospect Hill, 1919

VI-17
Great Falls, Scotts Run

173

[On some excursions to the Swinks Mill area on Scotts Run, the Rambler went north from the electric line station Hitaffer—where Old Dominion Drive (the path of the old electric railway to Great Falls) meets Swinks Mill Road.]

14 April 1918: [Hitaffer] *is a station on the Great Falls division of the Washington and Old Dominion Railway. . . . Close to the station of Hitaffer is one house sheathed partly with wide weather boards and partly with tin. It has been spruced up recently by a new owner and its garden is gay with fruit trees in blossom. It was the builder of this simple house who put the name Hitaffer on the map. He was John Hitaffer, a carpenter. . . . He built his house close by the side of an old road, which leads from Swinks mill on the Georgetown and Leesburg turnpike by way of Jones' Corners and Odrick schoolhouse, a distance of four miles, though a line three miles long would reach from one of these ancient turnpikes to the other* [Rt. 193 to Rt. 7]. *When the electric railway was built from the Aqueduct Bridge to Great Falls it was decided to make a stopping point where the railway intersected the road connecting the pikes.*

14 April 1918: *If you stand at Hitaffer and look to the southwest you will see, about 300 yards away, a house with a low sloping roof, dormer windows and a wide, deep porch. It is a house whose architecture and age and state of neglect will probably enlist your interest and sympathy. . . . The life story of this house reaches back to the youth of the United States.*

14 April 1918: *Below the southern edge of the garden* [of the Jackson House] *and by the side of a trail which leads from the barn to the old road* [Swinks Mill Road today] *there is a ruinous 'cabin.' Built of logs, the*

VI-18
Great Falls, House near Hitaffer, 1919

174

VI-19

Jackson House near Hitaffer, Va., 1919 [1157 Swinks Mill Road]

VI-20

*Log Cabin on Jackson Place
near Hitaffer, Va., 1919*

interstices were chinked with mortar mixed with bits of stone and brick. Most of this chinking has fallen out. . . . Time and weather have warped it so that its lines are considerably out of plumb. . . . [Charles Turner, the man in the photo No. 21, told the Rambler that he was an exslave from Fauquier County, and after the war worked at the Jackson-Cutts place for more than thirty-five years living in this log cabin when Samuel H. Cutts owned the property. Mr. Cutts "bought it from the Jacksons before the war."]

VI-21
Negro at Cabin Door
at Jackson Place near Hitaffer, 1919

VI-22
Road near Hitaffer, Va., 1919
[Swinks Mill Road]

The man who was buried [in the little burial ground close by his father's home, the Jackson House] *was a chief actor in the tragic episode at the beginning of the Civil War.* [On 24 May 1861, James W. Jackson, proprietor of the Marshall House in Alexandria, shot and killed the Union Col. Elmer Ellsworth when he removed the Confederate flag floating over the hotel. Jackson was then killed by the Colonel's men.]

21 April 1918: *Repassing the solitary house that marks the station Hitaffer, the ancient road, untouched by those men who made roads so good that only people with automobiles will use them, leads toward* [Swinks Mill and] *the wild lands that extend from the Georgetown and Leesburg Pike to the river. . . . There is nearly a mile of road from Hitaffer to the pike* [Rt. 193] *and at the intersection of these roads is Swinks Mill . . . and nearby is a small bit of the ruin of Ball's Mill.*

VI-23
House on Road to Swinks Mill
[Published caption:
"Jess Mason Home above Scotts
Run.'] 28 April 1918.

28 April 1918: *In the southwest angle* [of Rt. 193 and Scotts Run]
*is Swinks Mill, now used as a barn,
and with a mammoth wheel at its side.
It is a wheel that has not turned for
generations* [on the right side of the
building]. . . . *Scotts run . . . turned the
wheels of Ball's and Swink's mills . . .*
.

VI-24
Swinks Mill, Scotts Run
Great Falls, 1918

8 November 1914: *Across the run* [Scotts Run] *and up the hill on the westward side you pass over the paving of the old pike . . . heavy pieces of bluestone . . . a pavement rougher than the cobble paving of any backward city. At the top of the hill and on the right of the road is a picturesque ruin and the fragment of a ruin. The walls of a stone barn stand and the stone chimney of a house. These buildings were burned by Union soldiers early in the war. This was the farm of James Jackson,* [and "the home of the forefathers of the James Jackson who killed Col. E. E. Ellsworth."[5] James Jackson was buried on the Jackson/Cutts grounds, his wife near the stone ruin. Both were reinterred later in the cemetery at Fairfax village.[6] The rebuilt house at the Jackson ruins at 7728 Georgetown Pike is called the "Dower House."]

30 April 1916: *From the west side of the mouth of Scotts run a trail leads south and west up the timbered and rocky hillside. . . . On top of the ridge the trail passes a ruinous and abandoned house.*

VI-27
Great Falls
Abandoned House near Jackson, 1918

VI-25
Ruins of the Jackson Barn
Leesburg Pike [Rt. 193]

VI-26

[Trail] Road near Swinks Mill, Scotts Run

VI-29

Great Falls, Charcoal Burners' hut, 1915

30 April 1916: *Along the way a big black patch on the ground shows where charcoal burners have worked hard and long for a small return in money.* [Charcoal was produced by partially burning wood in large kilns or piles from which air was excluded.]

VI-28

Great Falls, Charcoal Burners', hut and mound, 1915

VI-30
Great Falls
Bull Neck Run, 1916

30 April 1916: *Across Bull Neck run and up the steep slope going west one passes through a district turned topsy-turvy by gold hunters, and many of the mines or prospect holes show fresh earth and newly broken rock. . . . A branch path leading to the north comes to an end at Prospect Rock.*

VI-32
Great Falls
Gold Washing

VI-31
Gold [mine]

180

VI-33
Great Falls
Prospect Rock

16 April 1916: [Prospect Rock] *is a mile west of the mouth of Scotts run . . . about one mile north of the pike.*

20 June 1915: *Prospect Rock is a rugged, rude-built tower on the Virginia side of the Potomac River. . . . No man's hand played any part in the building of this tower. It is older than any work of man. . . . Climbing upon the rocks, you have such a view of the river, the woods and the hills to the north, the east and the west as an eagle might envy.*

VI-34
Great Falls
Prospect Rock

VI-35
Great Falls
Camp – Louis Delano

20 June 1915: . . . *the land between the Leesburg Pike* [Rt. 193] *and the river is tree grown. . . . In these woods . . . is an occasional permanent home, bungalow or 'camp' but they are few.*

30 April 1916: *At the base of Prospect Rock the trail leads west through woods. . . . Out of the woods the trail leads into a long meadow. . . . Black pond . . . lies at the western end of the mead-ow. . . . Skirting the north side of Black Pond one passes through a tract of the roughest and in a way the most lovely country around Washington. There is a formation of rock, with very little soil, yet heavy . . . . The rock waste is 500 yards long and from 100 to 200 yards wide, and has an area of fourteen acres. Its southern end is at the mouth of Difficult run.*

VI-37
Great Falls
Rocks near Black Pond, 1921

VI-36
Great Falls, Black Pond

10 October 1915: *The region of Black pond and Difficult run . . . lies between Little Falls and Great Falls. . . . The point is about 1/3 of a mile long and 200 feet wide. It extends southeast from a point about 1/4 of a mile southeast of the mouth of Difficult run. . . . [It] is a dark pool with little water flowing in or out of it. . . . The pond is a body of water lying in a deep hole in what was formerly a part of the river channel.*

30 April 1916: *Difficult run, now wholly within Fairfax County, once formed a part of the boundary between that county and its offspring County of Loudoun [1757–1798]. . . . Its source is two miles west of the village of Fairfax. . . . It flows beneath the Alexandria and Leesburg pike 9 miles west of Falls Church, and under the Georgetown and Leesburg pike 8 miles west of Chain Bridge. Within one mile after passing the Georgetown and Leesburg Road, it enters the Potomac two miles below the Great Falls.*

19 May 1918: *Near the observation platform at Great Falls is a mass of gneiss set by nature in ledges. . . . On the west face of this rock heap is a bronze plate inscribed, 'In memory of George Washington of Fairfax County, Patriot, Pioneer, and Man of Affairs. He spent in Developing His Country, the Life He Risked in Her Defence. This is exemplified in the Potowmack Company, Incorporated to Build the Potowmack Canal, of which George Washington was the First President. Placed by the Fairfax Chapter, DAR.'*

VI-39
Great Falls
Looking up River at Mouth of Difficult Run

VI-40
Great Falls, River and Rocks

VI-41 and VI-42
George Washington Canal, Lock

VI-43
George Washington Canal

VI-44
George Washington Canal, 1907

VI-45
Great Falls Old Canal

VI-46
Great Falls
Ellen and Tom, Sept. 1921

VI-47
Great Falls, Rocks & Trees
Group of Walkers, 1921

[Great Falls Park was the last stop on the electric railway built from the Aqueduct Bridge to Great Falls.] 14 April 1918: *Between Hitaffer and Great Falls are the stations Jackson, Prospect Hill, Belleview, Glendale, Peacock, Fairview, Elkins and Dickeys Road.*

12 May 1918: *The trail from Great Falls to the point where the River Bend road ends at the Potomac is familiar to a good number of persons. . . .* [However] *It is very likely true that great numbers of Washington people have come to look on Great Falls as the end of the earth because it is the end of a trolley line, or at least they think of it as the frontier of civilization. . . . About a mile above the falls the Potomac swerves to the northeast and then, with a wide and leisurely bend, changes its direction to the west. That turn in the river is called 'the Bend'. . . . But above the falls . . . and back from the river are some of the fairest farms and happiest families in Virginia. It is a region of peace and great beauty.*

VI-48
Great Falls
Group (War Workers), 1921

188

Where the River Bend road enters that road which is simply called the 'county road' [Walker Road], and which leads from the Georgetown and Leesburg pike near Elkins to Deanwood, one comes upon a fine outlook. . . . Turning to the right into the county road, you will, after a walk of a few hundred yards, come within sight of an old house . . . which occupies the top of a knoll . . . the very high land of this locality . . . [from which] one gets a fine view . . . of Sugarloaf mountain. . . . Mountain View farm is one of several Turner farms in Fairfax County. John E. Turner was the founder of this family in Virginia . . . in 1840.

VI-49
Road
Great Falls Region, 1915
[The published photo caption is "A View of the River Bend Road." Another print caption is "Near Mountain View."]

Right: VI-49a
Mountain View Farm House, 1918

[Returning now to the area on both sides of Rt. 193 northwest of Swinks Mill and the Jackson ruins, Prospect Hill.] 21 April 1918: *Beyond that is high cleared land with houses set in clumps of trees with lines of cedars marking the course of a road. The tree-tops and the house-tops seem to touch the sky. That is Prospect Hill, the roof of the world in that part of the environs of Washington.* 5 May 1918: *The road leading across the hill is the familiar Georgetown and Leesburg turnpike . . . which is just a plain and rough county road. Along the east side of the hill flows Bull Neck run. . . . Along the west side of the hill flows Rocky run.*

5 May 1918: *The Carper family gave its name to this skyland, and all the people roundabout know it as Carpers Hill. They consider 'Prospect Hill' an imported name. . . .*

VI-49b
Great Falls
Group at Mountain View
Farm, 1918
[The published photo caption is "Some of The Turners of Mountain View Farm."]

Left: VI-50
Great Falls
Carper House on
Prospect Hill, 1919

VI-51
Leesburg Pike [Rt. 193]
(Summer Road)
Made at Crossing of
Carpers Hill Road and Pike
(Old Trammell Place)

Below: VI-52
Trammell House near Difficult Run
Great Falls, 1916

19 May 1918: *The first of the Trammells in this part of Virginia whose memory is preserved . . . was Dr. Trammell. He had a son named Washington Trammell. Washington Trammell's house is still standing near Carper's school in the Prospect Hill neighborhood between the Georgetown and Leesburg pike and the river. Washington had a son named John Trammell and the chimney of his ruined home stands a few hundred yards north of the pike at the north edge of Prospect Hill.*

VI-53
Great Falls
Barn on Trammell Place near Difficult Run, 1917

VI-54
Group on Prospect Hill at Trammell Place

192

Below: VI-56
Great Falls
Tolson Mill on
Difficult Run

16 June 1918: *Bellevue* [Bellview] *is a place name given to the intersection of Tolson Mill road and the railroad to Great Falls. . . .* [The railway station was northwest of Prospect Hill.] *Close to Bellevue are Spring Hill and Prospect Hill, and there one ought to get the impression that it is a hilly country. The road that crosses at Bellevue is the Tolson mill road. . . . It was laid down to lead from Alexandria pike to Tolsons mill, which stood on Difficult run between the Georgetown and Leesburg road and the river. The stone ruin of the mill is there yet and it is one of the most satisfactory ruins about Washington, that is, though it is a complete ruin, yet enough of the stone walls are standing to tell that it was a mill. . . . The Rambler has since learned that it was Tolsons mill before it was Walkers mill. . . .*

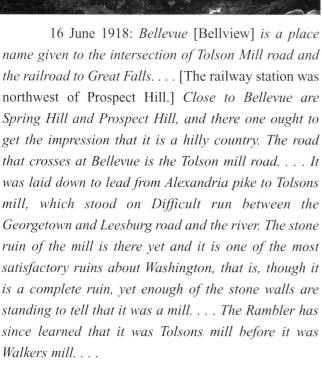

16 June 1918: *The road leading south from Bellevue* [Tolson Mill Road] *rambles along through a bit of country . . . called 'rolling' country and to which the word 'wild' . . . would not apply because the fields are too green and well-tilled, the orchards too bright and the old homes too numerous. . . .* [The Tolson Mill Road has become Bellview Road. Its path south to Route 7 appears today to have been intercepted by residential development. Only its last stub close to Route 7, from Brook Rd. in Woodside Estates, is designated as "Old Tolson Mill Rd.."]

[The next road off Rt. 193 northwest of Tolson Mill Road (Bellview Rd. today) is Route 676, so identified until c. 1957 when it was officially named Towlston.[7] The Rambler took this road.] 23 June 1918: *The landscape presented a succession of wheat and corn fields, but about a mile along and off to the right at the end of a long lane there is an old house so bowered in big locust trees that one must look closely to see that a house is concealed there. The top of a stone chimney—there are three of them—and a bit of shingle roof reaching down to form the cover of a long porch, betray it.*

It is the homestead of the Oliver family, one of the long-settled families in Fairfax county, and closely related to the Smith family. Fairfax county was young when this Oliver-Smith house was built. . . . On a hilltop about a hundred yards southwest of the Oliver house is the Oliver family burying ground . . . . Living in the Oliver house today is Octavia Oliver, eighty-two years old, daughter of James Oliver. . . . Temple Smith, who lives with his family in the old house . . . is a son of George Smith who married Mary Oliver. . . . It is not a long walk from the Oliver house to the site of old Union Church. . . .

VI-57
The Oliver Homestead
[From the published June 1918 article.
Today the Henry Mackall home at 1032
Towlston Road.]

30 June 1918: *Last Sunday the walk led past the site of Old Union Church, Bethel Church, which stands beside that site, and the farms which for generations have been tilled by the Smith and Oliver families. . . . Not a vestige of Old Union Church remains. . . .* [Bethel Regular Baptist Church at 1130 Towlston Road stands near the site.] *Off the road to the southwest one can see a gray old house that was the home of Temple Smith and his ancestors and is one of the historic houses near Washington—That is if a calm existence of a century and a half makes a house historic. . . . Temple Smith . . . married Sarah E. Oliver, and their [daughter] Annie Elizabeth married Lewis Cass Leigh, son of Alfred Leigh of Fairfax. . . .*

It was to visit this venerable Smith home that the Rambler made this trip. Early in the eighteenth century

VI-58
Temple Smith House 1918.
[Now known as Towlston Grange, the C. J. S. Durham house 1933–1996 at 1213 Towlston Road.]

there came to northern Virginia from England three brothers, George, Wethers and Temple Smith. They were rich men of good family. George had a son Samuel. . . . Samuel had a brother, James, and <u>*those boys built the house which the Rambler has in view.*</u> *Samuel succeeded to its ownership after James' death.* [And according to the Rambler, one of Samuel's sons was Temple Smith.]

[From Mr. Shannon's Rambler article and accompaning captioned photograph can be gleaned the information that the Temple Smith house and the house now known as Towlston Grange at 1213 Towlston Road are the same. Evidently and surprisingly, it was known only as the Temple Smith house to the Rambler, a generally very well-informed man. He would undoubtedly have written prolifically if he had known, or had heard in his conversations with the Smith descendants, that this house had been the home of Bryan Fairfax who in 1757 inherited the inclusive Northern Neck grant of 5568 acres called Towlston Grange, and became the 8th Lord Fairfax. The fact that in 1918 the Rambler <u>did</u> write that the house was built by the Smiths casts some doubt that it had been the manor house of Bryan Fairfax.]

VI-58a
*Temple Smith House
Fairfax County and Old
Woman, 1915*
[The published caption reads:
"Mrs. Lewis Cass Leigh and
Family." She
was the daughter
of Temple Smith.]

VI-59
Jackson's Mill, Forestville, Va., 1919

[Off Towlston Road north of Bethel Church, another county road strikes off to the north (Leigh Mill Road today).] 7 July 1918: *This road leads down into the valley of Difficult run. . . . A few rods further on, there showed through the rifts in the trees that fringe Difficult run the gray stone and wooden walls of an old mill. . . . Further back than anyone in Fairfax County seems to be able to remember, the old mill was called Trammell's mill . . . . After passing out of the possession of the Trammells, it seems to have become Jackson's mill, and the last miller of that name was Bob Jackson. . . . From Bob Jackson the mill passed into the possession of Dr. Alfred Leigh, father of the present Dr. Alfred Leigh. . . .*

VI-60
Jackson Mill
Peter Hunstein [a Dane who had lived in a "time worn house close by the mill" for a year.]

VI-61
Great Falls
Log House of Jonas Oliver
Difficult Run, 1918

7 July 1918: *From the mill it was a long walk to the forgotten graveyard which lies among the pines and boulders above Difficult run between the Georgetown road and the river. . . . Off the north side of the pike* [Rt. 193 where it begins its descent to Difficult run], *a trace of a road leads into the woods and toward the river. . . . Following this you come to a clearing* [and] *the log house of Jonas Oliver, son of Aaron and grandson of James . . . . Close by the home of Jonas Oliver is the old burying ground. . . . No tombstone marks the graves. . . .*

VI-62
Great Falls
Group – Jesse Cornwell and Jonas Oliver
Difficult Run

198

2 June 1918: [The hamlet of Forestville (known as Great Falls today)] *lies on the Georgetown and Leesburg Turnpike a mile and a half or two miles west of the station at Elkins on the electric line to Great Falls.* 26 May 1918: *The schoolhouse is near the east side of the village of Forestville, which has settled itself along both sides of the pike and whose homes are set in green gardens that are wide and deep. Near the school is a narrow road which carries only the traffic of the few families it services. It winds along between trees and bushes for half a mile or so and then comes to open farm land and the vista there unfolded is a wide-fronted house with a low, deep slanting roof and dormer windows. It was to visit this place that the Rambler had walked from the electric railway at Elkins . . . . It was certainly one of the old Gunnell houses. The Gunnell family was numerous in size in Fairfax County long before the American revolution, and consequently there are various ancestral Gunnell houses, some standing, some in ruins. . . .*

26 May 1918: *Near the house but very much nearer the barn, is a plot of ground densely upgrown with that member of the iris family called the blue flag.*

In this thick and rank mass of vegetation are two old brown tombs that are upright but the soil has nearly swallowed them . . .'In memory of Nancy Gunnell, daughter of William and Sarah Gunnell who was born the 13th of September 1796, and expired the 23rd of September 1822 in the 27th year of her age. . . .' The second stone . . . was inscribed 'In memory of Lewis Mix or Mickx who departed this life on the 27th of April 1824, about the 34th year of age.' [Lewis Mix was the husband of Elizabeth Gunnell, another daughter of William (1750–1820) and Sarah. Another tombstone marked the grave of William and Sarah's son, William (1785–1834).]

The Rambler paused for lunch at a fine spring which supplies the Gunnell-Jenkins home. . . . [He met J. F. Nicholas who lived in the area and had known John Gunnell when he had been Squire of Gunnells Run.] [In his 23 June 1918 article, the Rambler lists John Gunnell and Richard Gunnell houses in the Great Falls section of Fairfax County. Richard Henry Gunnell (1820–1893), a brother of John Ratcliffe Gunnell (1825–1906), lived at "Chestnut Thicket," property given to him by their father, George West Gunnell.[8]]

VI-63
Great Falls
Gunnell House, 1917
["Gunnell's Run," 600 Innsbruck Ave., Great Falls.]

VI-64

Great Falls, Gunnell House, 1917 [Could this be Chestnut Thicket?]

VI-65

Great Falls, Gunnell House, 1917

2 June 1918: *At Forestville, where the pike runs from the southeast to the northwest, is another road, the general course of which is north and south* [Walker Road]. . . . *The Forestville schoolhouse stands in a clump of white oaks a short way east of the crossing of the roads and a few yards west of the crossway is a small frame structure painted white and also standing in the shade of oak trees. . . . Painted on the front of the building is this legend, 'Salem M. P. Church, 1876.'*

VI-66
Salem Chapel at Forestville
[The Great Falls United Methodist Church on Georgetown Pike, completed in 1949, stands adjacent to the site of Salem Church.]

26 May 1918: *The Rambler traveled north* [on Walker Road] *for the purpose of calling at Arnon Chapel.* . . . [He] *came to a road junction* [at Arnon Chapel Road today] *where stands Arnon Chapel* [S.E. corner], *a neat plain frame structure over the front of* which is the legend, in big black letters: 'Arnon Chapel M. E. Church South, 1890.' South of the chapel and on the opposite side of the road leading to the pike at Forestville is Arnon cemetery.

VI-67
Great Falls, Va., Arnon Chapel, 1910
[After its merger with Salem Church in 1944, Arnon Chapel was sold to become a private residence.[9]]

Footnotes on Chapter VI

1. Irving Brant, *James Madison 1812–1836*,
    Bobbs-Merrill Co., 1961, pp. 306–307.
2. Rambler, 2 August 1914.
3. Ibid.
4. John Chichester Mackall, *McLean, Fairfax Co.,
    Va.*, Historical Society of Fairfax County, Va.,
    Inc., 1955, Vol. 4, p. 2.
5. Rambler, 13 June 1915.
6. Ibid.
7. Mrs. C. J. S. Durham, *Towlston Road*, Historical
    Society of Fairfax County, Va., Inc., Vol. 7,
    1960–61, p. 21.
8. Karen Washburn, *The Gunnell Family of Fairfax
    County*, The Historical Society of Fairfax
    County, Va., Inc., Vol. 20, pp. 65–66.
9. Moria Rafferty, *The History of Arnon Chapel in
    Great Falls, Va.*, The Historical Society of
    Fairfax County, Va., Inc., Vol. 16, 1980,
    p. 114.

VII-1

From the 1972 MLS Loudoun County Map surveyed and
drawn by Eugene M. Scheel

Chapter VII

Continuing from
Dranesville Northwestward

8 November 1914: *From Dranesville to Leesburg the road, passing through a less difficult country than between Langley and Dranesville, has been made over and automobile and farm wagons are turning their wheels.*

DRANESVILLE

21 July 1918: *The village of Dranesville is where the great west stage road roughly parallels the south shores of the Potomac and points the way from Washington to the Blue Ridge. . . .*

14 July 1918: *Dranesville is six miles west of the Potomac at Great Falls . . . two miles east of the boundary line dividing Fairfax and Loudoun counties . . . ten miles north by a little east of Fairfax Court House and thirteen miles northwest of Chain Bridge. These are map distances in an air line. . . .*

The junction of the Georgetown [193], Alexandria [7] and Seneca roads is on high land and it is appropriate to call this point the beginning of Dranesville, for on this high land stood the homestead of the Dranes, the family which gave this hamlet its name. . . . The ancient Drane house was long ago torn down and on the hill was built the Wheat house. . . . The view from this hill sweeps the valley of Sugarland run, which is a water course. . . .

VII-1a
Road – Leesburg Pike near Dranesville, Va., 1916

VII-2

Dranesville, chimney

14 July 1918: *Dranesville is a small settlement in the upper part of Fairfax county. Nearly all the houses are old, the church is old, the inn is old and many of its inhabitants are old people with long keen memories. It is not a closely grouped village, but is strung along the road with such wide intervals between its homes that a traveler has no means of telling at which point he reaches Dranesville or at which point he leaves it.*

A little west of Wheat's hill and on the left of the road . . . stands the school house, a few yards south of the church. . . . This bit of high land is called Church

hill. This little church . . . is sometimes called Liberty Church and sometimes the Dranesville M. E. Church South [built in 1857]. There was a church at that point in 1790. It was a small log structure and was built through the efforts of a pioneer Baptist preacher named James Reid.

28 July 1918: *On the right hand of this long and hard old road [Rt. 7] where it crosses church hill are two houses which are the homes of Dr. William B. Day and Dr. John T. Day.*

14 July 1918: *The oldest house in the Dranesville neighborhood and one of the oldest if not the oldest in Northern Virginia, is the homestead of the Coleman family. It was built not later than 1727. Every timber of the house was hewed, every shingle riven by hand and every nail made separately in the blacksmith*

VII-3
Dranesville
House on Sugarland Run
Coleman, 1917

shop. Out of the roof project a line of dormer windows and above it rises three stone chimneys. In Braddock's order book . . . is this reference: 'From Fairfax Court House to James Coleman's on Sugarland run, 12 miles.' That was written in 1755. [The Coleman House was located on what was the predecessor of Route 7 (south of the later Alexandria Leesburg Turnpike.]

VII-4
Dranesville
Group – Coleman, 1917
[The published caption: "Samuel Coleman, wearing hat in a group of his friends."]

21 July 1918: *At the west end of the straggling village [on Rt. 7] is an ancient inn. It has probably been serving refreshments considerably more than a century. As far back as the memory of the Rambler and his friends go it was Jackson's tavern. Then it became* William T. McFarland's tavern, and for thirty-six years has been kept by Samuel Jenkins. . . . 14 July 1918: *Thousands of persons traveling over the pike . . . have noticed close by the roadside, the dusty, swinging sign inscribed, Dranesville Hotel, S. Jenkins, Prop.*

VII-5

Old Jackson Tavern

[Dranesville tavern. In 1968 the Fairfax County Park Authority acquired the tavern, and in 1972 it was placed on the National Register.]

[The bridge over Sugarland Run is on Route 7 north of the Coleman House site on the Run.] 4 August 1918: *These branches start in the counties of Loudoun and Fairfax, blending their waters south of Herndon, and then, as Sugarland run, they pass under a very old and picturesque bridge of native red sandstone . . . over which goes the Leesburg pike, and thousands of people* *whir along that road in automobiles without catching more than a glimpse of the rugged balustrades of the bridge. It is a mile and a half west of Old Liberty Church at Dranesville and two miles east of Green Wood Chapel, a plain little house of worship which stands on the south side of the pike west of Daysville. . . .*

VII-7

Green Wood Chapel, M. E. Church South

4 August 1918: *A little further on* [west] *one comes to a settlement that is strung along the pike. Its name is Daysville* [Loudoun County]. *Presumably it is named after the Drs. Day who lived at Dranesville. . . . Down the hill and up a hill and one comes to a chapel which stands in a green grove of oaks and pines on the left side of the pike. A faded sign on the front of the building reads 'Green Wood Chapel, M. E. Church South, 1889. . . .' Close to Green Wood a red dirt road bordered by cedars and wild greenery strikes off toward the Potomac. . . . At the east end of Daysville a road leads to the left and if followed patiently will carry one to Sterling* [Rt. 637].

VII-8
Road, Daysville to River, 1917
Leads off from Chapel down to McCarthy lands.

VII-9
Road near Daysville Va., 1918 [The road to Sterling.]

11 August 1918: *From Sterling, a pleasant little town in Loudoun county, about two miles beyond the border of Fairfax, runs one of those red roads which are numerous in that part of Virginia. A section of this road is one of the main streets of the village. For about 200 yards from the railroad station the red road leads southerly, paralleling the iron tracks of the Bluemont line and then turns east with a slight inclination to the north. It passes a number of happy homes of Sterling,* *the village schoolhouse shaded by big trees and a little frame church. . . . Farther on it passes between two cemeteries. Half a mile to the east of the village the red road crosses, close to its source, the waters of Cabin branch. . . . Cabin branch tumbles its turgid current into Broad run, a mile and a half to the northwest, and Broad run . . . flows away to the Potomac crossing beneath the Leesburg pike two miles west of Daysville.*

VII-10

The Stone Bridge over Broad Run, Leesburg Pike
[*The wide creek and the deep valley it has scoured through the country are spanned by a stone bridge of beauty, age and endurance. 18 August 1918.*]

Just beyond where it crosses near the head of Cabin Branch, the red road forks—one fork continuing east in a jagged course and entering a very old road by which one may cross Sugarland run and journey to Dranesville. It was one of the highways between east and west long, long before the building of the turnpikes, the Georgetown and Leesburg, the Alexandria and Leesburg, and the Little River pike, in the early part of the nineteenth century. This older road along part of its course has been obliterated. . . .

18 August 1918: *The Rambler turned east along that historic road as far as the Lane-Bridges homestead. . . . The house was standing there a century and a half ago, and the road was an old and travel-worn highway when Sir Peter Halkett's regiment of British grenadiers, forming a part of Braddock's army, marched over it from Alexandria to Winchester in April 1755.* [In agreement, the 15 December 1905 *Fairfax Herald* reported that: "We can find nothing to justify the generally accepted belief that the road about one mile south of Fairfax known as 'Braddock road' was ever traversed by Gen. Braddock and his troops."]

11 August 1918: [The historic road south of Route 7] *has the appearance of a farm lane and it leads to the fresh-painted white house which the Rambler glimpsed far off. . . . The house looks bright and new but under the modern weatherboarding are oak beams that were rough-hewed from trees that stood on the site of the house. The joists are mortised and pegged. . . . In colonial days . . . this place was called Lanesville. It was so-called because a branch of the Maryland Lane family had taken up land there. Sometimes it was called 'the half-way house,' because it was half-way between Alexandria and Winchester. . . . Miss Keturah Lane became the wife of Benjamin Bridges. They inherited the property.*

VII-11
Lanesville, Bridges Lane, 1915

VII-12
Lanesville
Bridges' House
[I. H. Bridges was on mailbox.]

VII-13
Lanesville, Loudoun Co.
Bridges Place
Well House

VII-14

Lanesville, Bridges Group, 1918

The pike, [North of the Bridges home] *from Dranesville to Goose Creek, about ten miles further west, is as straight as an arrow with the exception of one very slight deflection . . . five miles west of Dranesville. With your eye you can follow the pike. . . .*

VII-15

Road, Alexandria and Leesburg Pike, 1915
[This photo shows the straightness of Route 7 to the west but its exact location is uncertain.]

214

VII-16
The Store at Ashburn, Va., 1915

Left: VII-17
Goose Creek
Group at Ashburn

Broad run is about five miles east of Goose creek [and the town of Ashburn is located between the two, several miles south of Route 7].

3 November 1918: *Ashburn is a railroad town on the Bluemont division of the Washington and Old Dominion railway, being the sixth station beyond Herndon. . . . Ashburn is a busy and prosperous place.* [Mentioned are the stores, grains and fertilizer warehouse, post office, and blacksmith shop.]

VII-18

Group near Ashburn

Right: VII-19

Goose Creek

John Hutchison and Bro., 1918

[*20 July 1919: When the Rambler was in the Ashburn
and Goose Creek neighborhood last summer and winter he
wandered across the Hutchison farm, which had been the
Quilly Bauckman farm. . . . 10 November 1918: John R.
and Thomas Hutchison . . . built the new house on the
crest of the low ridge, having removed to this farm from one
. . . popularly known in the Goose Creek country
as Hutchinsons Mountain.*]

216

VII-20

Belmont House, Leesburg Pike

3 November 1918: *One of the main roads of the county, called Ashburn road, leads from that town to the Leesburg pike entering it near the tollgate and quite close to Belmont Chapel . . . and to the Belmont House, the Ludwell Lee home. . . .* 1 December 1918: *The Rambler looked across fields to another low and rounded hill where a big house poked its heavy chimneys higher than the oaks and cedars and showed its gables, porch columns and bits of wall growth through the branches of leafless trees. That is the Belmont House.* [It was built by Ludwell Lee in 1799.]

[Across Route 7 from the Belmont House is "Coton" which the Rambler approached from Goose Creek.] 3 November 1918: *The Rambler turned eastward on the pike, crossed the high bridge over Goose creek, climbed the grade beyond . . . and came opposite a stone gateway through which a drive leads to one of the great modern houses in Virginia. Its place name is Coton farm. It was one of the Lee plantations numerous in this region. . . . Far back from the public road, the tall chimneys of the house rise above the tree tops and a wide portico and many windows look out between rifts of foliage.* [Original home was built in 1803 by Thomas Ludwell Lee.]

VII-21

Belmont House, Leesburg Pike

VII-22

Margaret Mercer Monument, Belmont, Va., 1919
[Margaret Mercer (d 1846) founded Belmont Chapel 1835,
kept an academy at Belmont House, and was daughter
of Gov. John Francis Mercer.[1]]

VII-24
Coton House of the Lees, 1918
On Leesburg Pike near Goose Creek
[This house burned March 1920—now the site of Xerox Corp.]

VII-23
Goose Creek – Coton
House of the Lees near, 1918

VII-25

*Old woman near
Belmont and Ashburn, Va., 1918*

[Miss Sarah Margaret Solomon's father, George Solomon, blacksmith and wheelwright, owned a small tract on the pike he had inherited from his father, William Solomon. This became part of Coton farm. 17 November 1918.]

20 October 1918: *A short distance this side of Goose creek the railway to Leesburg and Bluemont comes to a small station bearing the name of Belmont Park. At one time this place was the western terminus of the railroad.*

VII-26

*Goose Creek.
Stone House, Belmont Park*

VII-27

Goose Creek

Group near old mill

Goose creek is the largest Virginia stream which enters the Potomac between Washington and the Shenandoah river. . . . [It] enters the Potomac river fourteen miles west by north of Great Falls.

LEESBURG

VII-28

Leesburg, Va., Court House and County offices, 1910

221

VII-29

Confederate Monument, In Court House Square, [Leesburg Inn in background.]

VII-30

Leesburg, Va., [Market] *Street*

[Old Rt. 15 in front of Loudoun County Court House unseen on the right. Bank on the left.]

VII-31

Leesburg, Va., Academy (High School) [Destroyed by fire prior to the 1930s.]

VII-32

Leesburg, Va., Col. E. B. White's, Monument in Cemetery
["Lige" White's tombstone, Laurel Brigade,
Union Cemetery.]

VII-34

*Balls Bluff, [Clinton Hatcher
1840–1861
Co. F., 8th VA. Regt. CSA
Fell bravely defending his native state.]*

Left: VII-33

Balls Bluff, Cemetery at
[one mile northeast of Leesburg.]

29 August 1915: *Close to the railroad tracks at Harpers Ferry stands a monument. . . . The monument bears the simple inscription, 'John Brown's Fort.'*

VII-35

Harpers Ferry, John Brown's Fort, 1921

VII-36

Harpers Ferry, West Va., View through gorge, 1921

VII-37

Harpers Ferry, Street, 1921

It is at Harpers Ferry that the Potomac river, joined by the Shenandoah, broke its way through the Blue Ridge and the scenery has charmed, enthused or awed millions of men. . . . If, leaving the tip of the town where the two rivers meet, you pass along the main street paralleling the Shenandoah river and which is called Shenandoah street—you ascend the first steep street to the right, you will note on the left hand a staircase of several broad and crooked flights, irregularly and roughly hewn out of the solid rock which form the hill. The dominating note in the picture at this point is a stone church, and it is to this church that the rock hewn stairway leads. . . . It is St. Peters Catholic Church . . . erected October 15, 1830; rebuilt October, 1896.

VII-38
Harpers Ferry, Rock Stairway, 1910–1921

VII-39
Harpers Ferry, Catholic Church, 1921

228

VII-40
Harpers Ferry, High School, 1921

Left: VII-41
*House on Road from Harpers Ferry
to Kennedy farm, 1912*

229

VII-42
John Brown
House on Kennedy farm
above Harpers Ferry

Bottom Left: VII-43
John Brown
Group on Kennedy Farm
above Harpers Ferry

Bottom Right: VII-44
John Brown
Woman Who Knew Him
Kennedy farm, 1910
6 miles from Harpers Ferry

230

VII-45
Harpers Ferry, W. Va.
Jefferson's Rock

VII-46
Harpers Ferry
Robert Harper's Tomb, 1910
[The founder of Harpers Ferry
Born 1713 Died 1782]

VII-47
Charlestown, W. Va.
Street, 1921

Right: VII-48
Shepherdstown, W. Va.
Church, 1913

VII-49
Front Royal, Va.
Court House

VII-50
Front Royal, Va.
Group at Court House, 1921

Right: VII-51
Front Royal, Va.
Street Scene

VII-52

Front Royal, Va., Post Office and Opera House, 1921

VII-53

Confederate Monument, Front Royal, Va., 1921

235

VII-54

Harrisonburg, Va., Court House, 1921

[Harrisonburg, the *"Hub of the Valley,"* is the seat of Rockingham county. This towered granite courthouse still standing on Court Square was built in 1896, the fifth court building since 1781[2]]

236

Above: VII-55

Harrisonburg, Va., Post Office, 1921

[The first unit of the old Post Office building opened in 1886. The new Post Office was built in 1940.[3]]

VII-56

Harrisonburg, Va., Town Sergeant, 1921

[at the Post Office.]

VII-57
Harrisonburg, Va., Episcopal Church, 1921
[The old Emmanuel Episcopal Church building was erected on the corner of Bruce and South Main Streets in 1868. It was used by the congregation until 1960.[4]]

VII-58
Harrisonburg, Va., Baptist Church, 1921

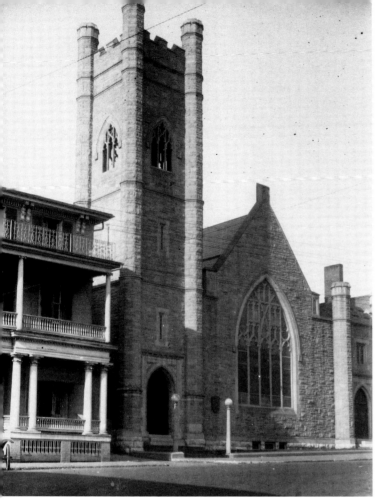

VII-59
Harrisonburg, Va.
Presbyterian Church, 1921
[The First Presbyterian Church was organized in 1789
fifteen days before Gen. George Washington
was inaugurated as the first President of the United States.[5]]

VII-60
Harrisonburg, Va., High School, 1921

VII-62

Harrisonburg, Va., Streets, 1921

Footnotes on Chapter VII

1. Richardson Index, pp. 108–109.
2. WPA, p. 425.
3. Harrisonburg-Rockingham Historical Society.
4. Ibid.
5. Ibid.

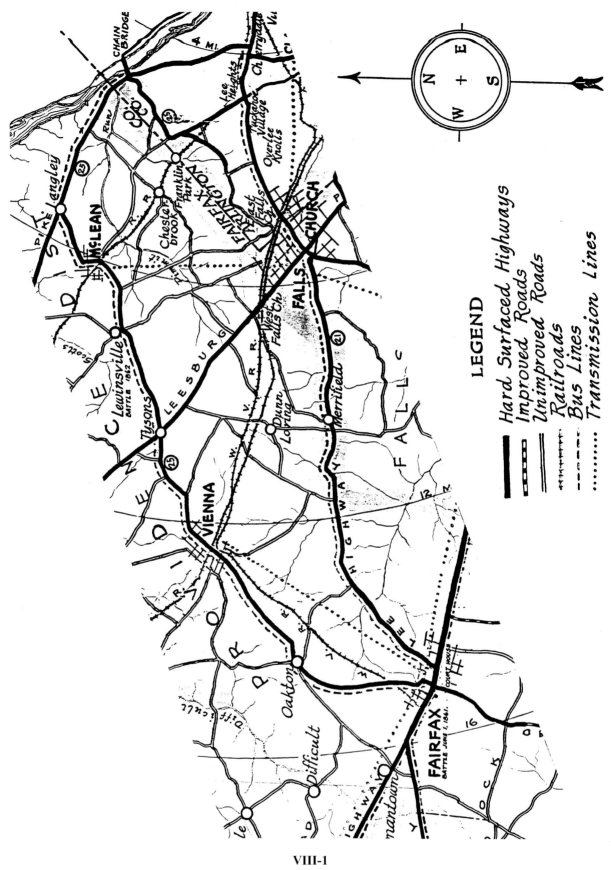

VIII-1

"A Map of Fairfax County, Virginia" published July 1927 by the Fairfax County Chamber of Commerce.
Courtesy of D. Barton Betts.

Part 3. Over to Bull Run

Chapter VIII

Leaving Langley for Points West

2 August 1914: *You do not follow the Leesburg Pike* [Rt. 193] *west of Langley, but turn to the south on the fair dirt road* [Chain Bridge Rd.] *which leads to Lewinsville, Tyson Cross Roads, Freedom Hill, Vienna, Fairfax Court House and many other places. Soon after branching into this road at Langley you see on the left a large red brick house with a mansard slate roof, situated on a low green hill. . . . The place is called Hickory Hill* [1147 Chain Bridge Road]. . . . *At the next farm on the left a long lane leads to a frame house* [Anchorage].

Farther along and the next farm on the left, you catch a glimpse of the gables of a brick house, a chimney and part of a gray shingle roof. A mass of foliage nearly shuts the house from view.

A straight lane, about a quarter of a mile long, leads from the main road to this house. . . . It runs directly through the wheat field. You draw up in front of the garden which surrounds the house. A whitewashed fence four board high incloses the garden. Inside are old cedars thick through the truck and solemn in foliage. . . . A driveway curves to the left and a gravel path leads straight to the front porch, before which big

box trees are growing. The porch is capacious with a balcony on top. Under the porch and in the middle of the house is an arched doorway. . . . This is Salona. It is a fine, quiet and dignified old place. . . . Salona was built by Rev. William Maffitt in 1801.* [Salona at 1235 Dolley Madison Blvd. is the house that sheltered President James Madison the night of August 24, 1814 when the British burned public buildings in Washington, D.C., including the White House.]

7 January 1917: *Langley's nearest neighbor-settlement is McLean, a new railroad village, lively and prosperous on the electric line to Great Falls . . . nearly a mile and three-quarters by the road which runs west by south and then turns south.* [Between Langley and McLean stands Salona, about half a mile from McLean, "a new and prosperous village."[1]]

7 January 1917: . . . *a few years ago the church building was hauled across the fields from Langley and set up on a new foundation in the village of McLean. It is St. John's Church.* [This frame Episcopal church was originally erected at Langley, then moved to McLean in 1908 on Chain Bridge Rd. near the electric trolley line (Old Dominion Dr.).]

VIII-1a

Salona, Front view

VIII-2

St. John's Church and Rectory, McLean, 1917

[Only the Rectory (now Zenias Boutique) stands
today at 1389 Chain Bridge Road.]

24 December 1916: *The Rambler again went out to McLean [on the trolley] and walked to Lewinsville. It is a cross roads settlement, with a store, blacksmith's shop, dwelling and church at the junction* [of Chain Bridge Rd., Great Falls Rd. and Lewinsville Rd.], *but with a number of well kept and prosperous-looking farmhouses close by. . . . Off the north side of the road* [Chain Bridge] *is a little church surrounded by solemn cedars and somber spruces. Behind it are the graves of hundreds of people who once worshipped there. . . . The church, a plain frame building, sits on a rough rock foundation apparently much older than the superstructure. . . .*

3 January 1915: *In the cemetery of the Presbyterian Church at Lewinsville, he came upon the grave of Parson Maffitt, who opened his home, Salona, to President and Mrs. Madison when Washington was in the hands of the British.* [It is now thought that Mrs. Madison spent the night at Rokeby.] *It was this parson, so the Rambler was told at Sharon, whose daughter became the wife of Commodore Jones, and who married the couple . . . .* [At Salona, Commodore Jones married Mary Walker Carter, the stepdaughter of the Rev. Mr. Maffitt.[1a]]

8 November 1914: [At the Lewinsville cemetery] *The Rambler strolled over to a big weeping willow. . . . Close to it . . . was a plain old fashioned headstone of marble: Commodore ap. Catesby Jones, United States Navy . . . died at Sharon, Fairfax County, Va., May 30, 1858.*

VIII-3
Lewinsville Presbyterian Church where Commodore Jones is buried

31 December 1916: *The road from Lewinsville to Tysons Crossroads . . . crosses Scotts run near its source, about a mile west of Lewinsville. Near the point where the road and run intersect, you will, if you travel that way, see, on land higher than the road and about 200 yards off the north side of it, a big frame house whose gray and long weathered boarding will tell you that it is a venerable home. . . .*

A narrow lane, bordered on both sides with tall and hoary locust trees with its banks matted with periwinkle and other vines, leads from the main road to the house. It is a big house, two stories high, with an ample garret and a wide deep cellar. . . .

The gray house on the hill [was called Strawberry Vale. The families Scott, Lee and Gantt were the early successive owners. For details see the Stuntz book, *This was Tysons Corner.*[2]]

VIII-4
Strawberry Vale Manor, 1916

VIII-5

Road to Strawberry Vale Manor, 1915

24 December 1916: [Leaving Strawberry Vale, the Rambler proceeded westerly on Chain Bridge] *until his road intersected the Alexandria and Leesburg turnpike, and that road junction, after a family which owned land there long before the Civil War, is called Tysons Cross Roads. . . . The purpose of the Rambler was to visit the site and debris of a Civil War signal station and stockade which stood at Tysons Cross Roads on some very high land in the northwest angle of the road from Langley to Vienna and the Alexandria and Leesburg Pike.*

The hill rises to a height of 500 feet above sea level and overtops all the other high land in that vicinity. . . . The land is encumbered by a plentiful supply of brush, but if you know the way you will find remains of the signal tower and the stockade, nearly all fallen to the ground and rotted, but here and there an upright pole to mark the line of the wooden wall. Through a section of the woodland runs an abandoned road, picturesque in its roughness and loneliness. It was a section of the wartime road which led from Langley to Tysons Cross Roads. . . .[2a]

VIII-6

Wood scene on Observatory Hill, 1912

[This is now the Tysons Corner area encompassing the communication tower, the Falls Church water tower, and Clydes Restaurant.]

24 December 1916: *At the crossroads are a store and the storekeeper's dwelling. The merchant, S. E. Myers, and her family live there.* . . . [They] *bought the place from John Core, who bought it from Tyson.*

6 October 1912: *Tysons Corners is a store embellished with legends assuring all who read that tobacco, starch, soap, bluing, horse liniment and poultry food advertised by those signs is the best on earth. Next to the store is the storekeeper's dwelling. The buildings were owned and occupied during the civil war by a family named Tyson. Prior to and during the war this junction of the roads was called Peach Grove. Tysons Corners is not far from Great Falls, and a good many autos and cycle tourists out of Washington travel to the Falls that way. Hence Tysons Corners is of local interest.*

VIII-7
Abandoned road to Stockade Hill, 1914

VIII-8
[Not a Rambler's photo. Tyson/Myers Store circa 1920, Courtesy of John Myers Sherwood. When the Rambler visited in 1912–1916, the store was bereft of the side addition which was built circa 1920. The dwelling house is barely visible recessed to the right of the store.[3]]

248

14 September 1919: *A few days ago the Rambler stopped at the picturesque village of Vienna, which* [partially] *stands on the tract which John Hunter, the Scottish immigrant, bought* [1776] *and named Ayrhill.*[4]

Resting in the shade of the railroad station, the Rambler opened a conversation with [several citizens he met].

In the course of his search for information, the Rambler walked into the store of L. L. Freeman—Leon Lydecker Freeman—one of the annalists of the Vienna neighborhood, but Mr. Freeman was in Washington. Freeman's store is one of the landmarks of that part of Fairfax county. In pioneer days [built in 1859] *in Vienna it was Lydecker's store. Lydecker came to Virginia from the Ramapo mountain region of New York* [N.J.?]. *L. L. Freeman is the grandson. . . .*[5]

VIII-10
Vienna, Va., Store and Man, 1919
[Leon Lydecker Freeman (1872–1941)]

VIII-9
Lydecker-Freeman Store

249

15 July 1917: [On an earlier trip, after passing Tysons Cross Roads, the Rambler reaches Vienna.] *Walking along the main way of Vienna, which is the automobile road leading directly southerly to Fairfax Court House* [Maple Avenue], *he turned eastward into a narrow road with green and shrubby boarders which is called 'Old Court House Road.' This road is so-called because it is the older road leading from Vienna to the village of Fairfax. . . . Broad fields stretch away to distant woods. Some of the fields are fruitful with corn and wheat, and some are set off in orchards. Others are white with daisies. . . .*

16 November 1919: *. . . the Rambler turned his footprints from Old Courthouse road and entered upon a lanelike way leading east. . . .* 15 July 1917: [This lanelike way] *crosses fields and comes to a gray and rambling house where the porch is covered with fragrant white magnolia roses and great purple flowers of clematis. This is the Broadwater house, the Virginia ancestral home of quite a celebrated family.* 5 October 1919: *This is the manor house of Springfield. It was built in* [circa] *1750* [by Col. Charles Broadwater]. *Part of the house has disappeared . . . .*[6]

VIII-11
Oldest Part of the Broadwater House [Springfield.]

VIII-13
Road to Hunter place, 1920 [Moidon]

VIII-12
"Springfield", Broadwater House, Vienna
[The newest and last section of Springfield
which was demolished in 1985. It stood at
S.W. corner of Tapawingo and Frederick streets.]

16 November 1919: [The lanelike way (the old
Frederick St.) continues eastwardly past the south side
of Springfield] . . . *it passes close to the south side of
the long and rambling house of Springfield, where colonial box bushes grow. . . . Then it leads . . . through an
arcade of locust and walnut trees. . . . In the distance,
on a ridge to the east, you see a plain house whose
weatherboards are gray.*

[George Washington Hunter, Sr., inherited 1/2
of Springfield from his maternal grandfather, Col.
Charles Broadwater. He built Moidon in 1806. In 1836,
he and his wife transferred Moidon to their son, Dr.
James Hunter. Col. and Mrs. George W. Hunter then
moved to an adjoining property which later became
known as the Margaret Hunter House, named for
their daughter, Margaret Hunter, who inherited the
property.[7]]

VIII-14

Hunter House (Moidon), near Vienna, Va., John Boyle, 1919

[A friend of the Rambler by the kitchen of Moidon with the main house showing to the left.]

VIII-15

*Hunter (Margaret),
House near Vienna*

252

VIII-16
Group Near, Margaret Hunter place, 1919
[Published photo: "Group living at Hunter House."]

15 July 1917: *From the garden of the home* [Springfield] *there is visible across the fields to the east the home of Jeremiah Moore* [(1746–1815), the pioneer Baptist preacher]. *Over these fields the Rambler went, then under the shade of a grove of oaks, over a little stream and into a country road that connects with the Old Court House Road. Opening a farm gate, he sauntered along the rough road bordered by big trees. . . . This is the private road through the lands of Moorefield, for that is the name of the home of Jeremiah Moore. . . . The Rambler came to a long low frame house. . . . In spite of its age or because of its age, it is a beautiful place.*

VIII-17
Spring House
Moorefield, near Vienna
[It was just to the west of Nutley Rd. at Tapawingo.]

253

VIII-18

The Moorefield [Now stands in the Townes of Moorefield at 900 Moorefield Hill Court, S.W..]

VIII-18a

Moore-Hunter House

VIII-19

Moorefield House of Jeremiah Moore near Vienna [rear view.]

VIII-20

Moorefield, Cline and Family, Group who owns place now, 1915 [In front of the well house.]
[*"Moorefield is now the property of F. H. Cline, whose wife was Florence Moore"* (a great-great granddaughter of Jeremiah Moore who owned Moorefield from 1902–1919).]

VIII-21

Children of Moorefield
The Hunter-Moore House
[at the front porch.]
[James Hunter (1818–1894) from Banff, Scotland,
and his family owned Moorefield from 1874 to 1902.
They called it Bothwell.]

VIII-22

Road to Hunter Place near Vienna, 1920
[This could be the long lane that led to Contemplation,
another Hunter home the Rambler wrote about on 10 August
1919: *"The John Chapman Hunter (1762–1849) farm,
Contemplation, lies south of Vienna on the road to Fairfax
Courthouse [Rt. 123]—a fine old home . . . ."* It stood, before
burning in 1973, on the back portion of the Mosby Landing
Condominiums near James Madison High School.]

16 August 1914: [The Rambler approached Falls Church via the route that is known as Lee Highway.] *Beginning at the Virginia end of the Aqueduct Bridge is another of the old roads of northern Virginia. It will lead you through Falls Church, a town of interesting historic import, but the historic atmosphere has been somewhat overwhelmed of late by saw,* hammer, *progress, and the influx of newcomers. It is one of the handsome and thriving suburbs of Washington and smells more of fresh paint and new plaster than of old ivy and ancient mold. That road passes on by the old church from which the town of Falls Church takes its name and leads to Fairfax Court House.*

VIII-23
Falls Church

VIII-24

Tree – Persimmon near Falls Church, 1917

Below: VIII-25

House, Haunted
(Crutchet Place near Falls Church)
[Still standing in 1998, this brick circa 1807 house,
covered with stucco after 1925, is located off W.
Great Falls Street near its intersection with Haycock Road.]

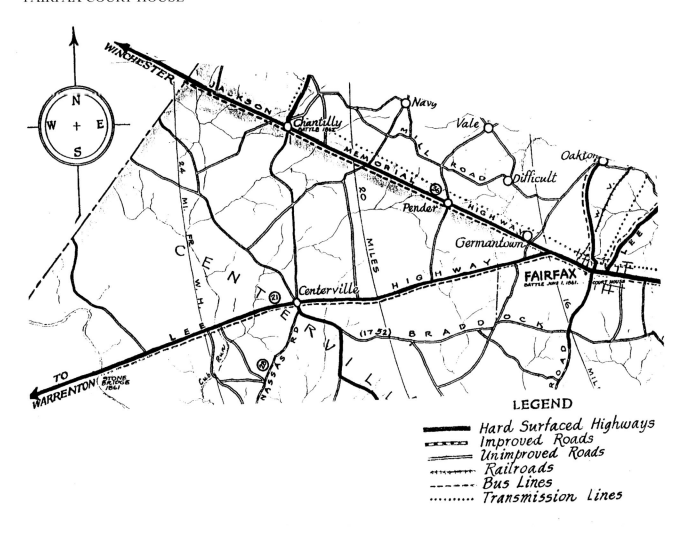

VIII-25a

"A Map of Fairfax County, Virginia" published July 1927 by the Fairfax County Chamber of Commerce.
Courtesy of D. Barton Betts

16 August 1914: *The village of Fairfax Court House is an interesting place to visit. . . . It is not the first court seat of Fairfax County. The court building at Fairfax though is old and historic . . . built in 1800. In the grounds of the courthouse is a handsome monument to Capt. Marr of the Warrenton Rifles who was killed a few rods south of the court building, and was the first soldier killed in action in the Civil War.* [He was the first Confederate Officer killed in action in the Civil War.]

VIII-26
Fairfax Court House,
1907

VIII-27
Fairfax Court House, 1907

VIII-28
Monument at Fairfax
[The John Quincy Marr Monument
was dedicated in 1904.]

Left: VIII-29
Fairfax Court House
Negro at Marr's Monument, 1916

261

VIII-30

Fairfax Court House, Negro who Found Capt. Marr's body

VIII-31

Fairfax Court House, Confederate Monument, 1912,
[This monument was erected in October 1890 in the
Fairfax Town Cemetery.]

Below: VIII-32

Fairfax Court House, Adam's Hotel, 1909
[Also known as the Willcoxon Tavern, this building
stood on the N.W. corner of the Rt. 236/Rt. 123 intersection
across Main Street from the Court House. The site is now
a branch of Nations Bank at 10440 Main St. In 1932, the
tavern was demolished and its bricks were used to build
the Francis Pickens Miller home in Oakton which became
Flint Hill Private School.]

VIII-33
Fairfax Court House, Street Scene

VIII-34
Fairfax Court House, Man and Team, 1910

264

16 October 1921: *A few rods west of the village of Fairfax, the Pike [Rt. 236, Main St.], rough and rutty in the olden time and now so hard and smooth that it is a speed course, crosses a stream. . . . As the Rambler came to the crossing of the Pike and Accotink Creek, a* horse, surrey, boy and dog came along. The boy was Christian Hockman, thirteen years old. [The Rambler rode with the boy] *to where the Warrenton pike [Rt. 29] turns off from the Little River turnpike [Rt. 236 at Kamp Washington].*

VIII-35
Centerville
Horse and buggy of Christian Hockman, 1921

VIII-36
Centerville, Va.
Mr. and Mrs. Greenberry Cronk, 1922
[Greenberry Cronk . . . *lives by the side of the Warrenton pike* in the Accotink Creek vicinity.]

265

CENTREVILLE

[The following group of photographs are also labeled Centerville—not Centreville as is seemingly now preferred. However, the 1792 Act of the General Assembly designated the town as Centerville.[8]]

16 August 1914: *It is a rough road. The Warrenton turnpike* [Rt. 29] *before the war was one of the fine roads of the county. It was 50 feet wide, hard and fairly smooth, but hilly. Now it is one of the worst. After the incoming of railroads it was somewhat neglected. During the Civil War it was altogether neglected, so far as repairs were concerned, and was pounded and rutted and worn and gullied by the army trains—artillery, quartermaster and commissary—for four years. . . .*

In a dip between hills you pass a little village strung along both sides of the road. It has the curious name of Legato, with the stress on the second syllable. It used to be famous for a distillery, not operated now, though the old building remains. Ridge after ridge and valley you cross for seven Virginia miles out of Fairfax, and a mile before you reach the end of your walk, you see a cluster of houses perched on high land. That's Centerville.

VIII-37
Warrenton Pike and Legato

VIII-38
Centerville, Va.
Man met on road

VIII-39
Centerville
Old Negro on Road

VIII-40

Centerville, Boy walked with, John Thomas Behn, October 1921, [Rambler's 13 year old walking companion on Warrenton Rd. to Centreville where John lived with his grandfather, J. W. Behn.]

VIII-41

Centerville
Colored Group on Warrenton Pike

Coming upon the ridge on which it stands you get your first view of a line of mountains, which at that distance, appears to rise steeply from the low but hilly lands that lie for miles around. That ridge is sometimes called Bull Run mountains. . . . It is about 12 miles away

16 August 1914: *Centerville is not a stirring place. . . . It is stagnant and drowsy. . . . If ever a village was killed in war it was Centerville . . . . Today it bears wounds and scars. . . . A dozen homes compose the hamlet. Half of them cling to the roadside, as though to feed their lean and leaning sides on such excitement as a passing team and the visitation of a stranger bring.*

VIII-42
Centerville, Va., Street

VIII-43
Centerville, Street

VIII-44
Centerville, Abandoned House, 1907

VIII-45
Centerville
House in Ruins
1916

VIII-46
Centerville, Va.
[Houses face the main road
through town, Braddock Rd.,
Rt. 620.]

9 October 1921: *At the end of main street* [near where Rt. 128 and Braddock Rd. meet] *and at the farther edge of the village is a little brownstone church which was a military hospital for men maimed in battle. . . .*

[This Stone Church at 13941 Braddock Road is known as Centreville Methodist Episcopal Church. The walls of the 1854 church were torn down between 1862 and 1865, but rebuilt in 1870.[9]]

VIII-47
Centerville, Va.
Stone Church, 1916

Right: VIII-48
Centerville
Stone Church, 1921

[At the time of Fig. 49, this house, situated close to Braddock Road, was known as the Red House because it was painted red. It was built circa 1790 and became a home and store/post office/hotel until the Fall of 1921. Advertising signs are evident in the next photo just before the Red House became only a family home. Shortly after Fig. 50 was taken, the house was purchased by Howard H. Havener—16 November 1921—and became known as the Havener House.[10]]

VIII-49
Centerville, Va.
House Nearly Opposite,
Stone Church, 1902

VIII-50
Centerville, Va., Old house,
Oct. 1921

9 October 1921: *A hundred yards from the little Methodist church, three brick chimneys rise above a jungle of paper mulberry trees and bushes. Until recently four chimneys were there, but one has fallen. The chimneys and the jungle growth mark the site of a house which was headquarters of a general whom the north looked on at first with hope and confidence and then with disappointment. . . . That was the famous Four Chimney House. It was a big frame house and from its windows and porches one commanded an enrapturing prospect north and west. The house fell into a state of shabbiness and unrepair thirty years ago. About ten years ago all the woodwork had disappeared and four tall chimneys remained.*

That house with its broad outlook over fields that were to be smoky and bloody, was the headquarters of McDowell in July 1861.

VIII-51
Bull Run
Four Chimney House at Centerville made in 1902, McDowell's Headquarters before 1st Manassas

VIII-52
Ruined Four Chimney House, Oct. 1921

VIII-53

Centerville, (Bull Run)

Pope's Headquarters after 2nd Manassas, made about 1902

9 October 1921: *Back from the dusty street* [Braddock Road], *on a green hillock and closely grown around and overshadowed by tall old locust trees is a big frame house* [Royal Oaks] *which was headquarters for another Union General from whom the North expected victory and realized defeat. Nearby are other houses and a plain and pretty little Episcopal church. . .*

16 August 1914: *The Civil War threw such a glare upon the hamlet* [of Centreville] *that the eyes of the world were drawn to it. Great legions of the Union and great armies of the Confederacy grappled around the town. . . . Centerville was a war-racked village over which one army and then another rolled. . . . Four sign-boards posted at the crossroads where the village stands tell the way. One reads 'To Bull Run, 3 miles.' The legend on another one is: 'To Chantilly, 4 miles.' A third is inscribed: 'To Aldie, 12 miles.' A fourth points to Fairfax Court House, seven miles away. These are names that thrill.*

276

VIII-54

Centerville, Group and Old Earthwork

VIII-55

Centerville, Va., Group of Children

Left: VIII-56

Centerville, Va.

Old Man, Oct. 1921

16 August 1914: *You will walk around the dusty single street of Centerville. The view of the surrounding country is fine. Westwardly leads your road [Rt. 29 or Warrenton Road],* and you look out over the fields through which flow Cub run, Bull run, Youngs branch— fields over which every regiment in Virginia marched and fought.

VIII-57
Bull Run, Stone Bridge, 1902

VIII-58
Bull Run, Scene near Stone Bridge

278

VIII-59

Bull Run, Stone House, 1900

VIII-60

Bull Run, Road to Sudley, 1902

VIII-61

*Bull Run, Sudley
Church, 1907*

26 July 1914: *What the Rambler would tell is the story of two small brownstone monuments which stand on the reddest parts of that once corpse-strewn region, monuments which . . . were built by the Union soldiers, still under arms, to the memory of their comrades who fell there and while those comrades' skulls* and skeletons still lay all around. These Bull run monuments were not only the first monuments of the Great War, but the only ones erected by the soldiers themselves—'In Memory of The Patriots Who Fell.' One of these monuments, twenty feet high stands on the Henry hill. The other monument, 16 feet high was located on the Groveton farm.

VIII-62
Bull Run, Henry Hill, Monument, 1900

26 July 1914: T*he owner of the Henry house at the time of the first battle was Mrs. Judith Henry* [widow of Dr. Isaac Henry]. *She was bedridden and* was killed in the early part of the fighting by a shell from Ricketts battery, which pierced the frame house and burst in Mrs. Henry's room.

VIII-63

Bull Run, Henry House, 1902

VIII-64

Bull Run, Henry Field

VIII-65

Bull Run, Stonewall Jackson's
Line of 1st Battle

Below: VIII-66

Primitive sketch of the Bull Run Area

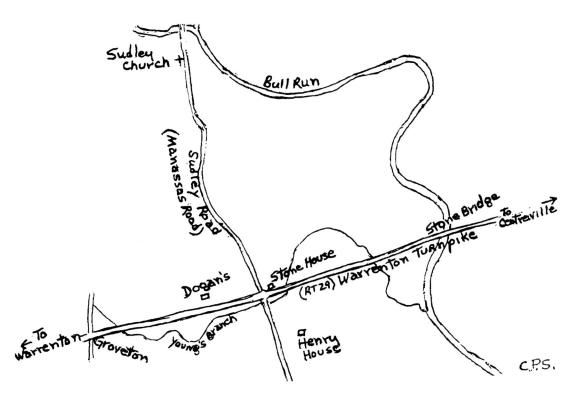

26 July 1914: *At the time of the first and second battles the Groveton lands were owned by Mrs. Dogan, a widow with several children. The Rambler had the honor of an acquaintance with old Mrs. Dogan [Lucinda Dogan 1817–1910]. Many battlefield remembrances has the Rambler written with that old woman sitting by him in the pleasant frame house at the junction of the Warrenton Pike and Sudley road. . . .*

24 January 1915: *Mrs. Dogan lived at Groveton, the bloodiest, ghastliest point of the second battle of Bull run. She owned the Peach Tree farm and the land through which that part of the railroad cut ran where was the heaviest fighting. . . . She was living there with her brood of children when Jackson and Lee and Pope met in one of the long and fierce encounters of the Civil War. When the guns ceased, she, with her daughters carried water by the bucket to the wounded men who, writhing and moaning among the dead, thickly strewed her fields.*

VIII-67
Bull Run
Looking West to Groveton
[Mrs. Dogan's farm facing Warrenton Road is on the right.]

VIII-68

Bull Run

Mrs. Dogan, Daughter Mollie and grandchildren, 1902

[Left to right: unknown, Dora Dogan, unknown, Lucy Senseney Dogan, Lucinda Dogan, Esther Terrill and Mollie Dogan]

286

VIII-71
Bull Run, Landscape

CHANTILLY

[As the signboard in Centreville noted, Chantilly was 4 miles to the north. The Rambler, however, traveled to Chantilly from Fairfax Court House via Little River turnpike (now Rt. 50 west from Kamp Washington), passing Jermantown where Jermantown Rd. crosses Rt. 50 today.]

Left: VIII-72
Chantilly
Road near Jermantown, 1921

287

VIII-73

Chantilly, House on Pike

[The published photo is captioned: "Robey House On Little River Turnpike." The house stood across from the photographed lane in Fig. 72. It was bought by S. S. Robey in 1856. Son Rodolphus Robey lived there in 1921.]

30 August 1914: *Some distance out of Fairfax, as the Rambler recalls it was about 2 miles, you cross a big branch and a picturesque stone bridge. There is not much water in the creek, but the banks, the width of the bed, and the height of the bridge showed that in time of storms a flood roared and whirled there. . . . The Rambler was told it was Difficult creek. . . .*

VIII-74
Chantilly
Bridge over Difficult Run,
1921

288

Passing this creek, the next thing of interest along the way is a cross-road village named Pender.

The Rambler went on to Chantilly village, though it is like all the other hamlets or wayside hamlets in that part of the land—a general store, a blacksmith shop with a strange assortment of jumbles of delapidated buggies and wagons and two or three dwellings.

30 August 1914: *From Chantilly, the Rambler retraced his steps to Pender and turned southerly along a road* [West Ox Road] *leading over to the Warrenton Pike* [Rt. 29]. *Half a mile along he came to a farm gate with the name 'John N. Ballard' on it, and turned into a long lane to a home deeply veiled by the foliage of large trees. Capt. Ballard and his wife were on the broad and cool veranda.*

VIII-75
Village of Chantilly, Stable, 1906

VIII-76
Chantilly, Va., Ox Hill Farm, 1914
[The published caption reads, "Capt. John N. Ballard Owner
of Chantilly Battlefield and Mrs. Ballard."]

VIII-77
Ballard House, On Chantilly Battlefield
[The Thrift/Ballard home stood on the west side of West Ox
Road north of Route 66.]

30 August 1914: *Most of the fighting of the battle of Chantilly was on this farm, about five miles east of the village of Chantilly. . . . The Confederates called the fight the battle of Ox Hill that being the old name of the rising ground of the Ballard farm and where the settlement of Pender stands.*

At the time of the battle, the Ballard farm was called Thrift farm. Mrs. Ballard was Miss Thrift [and] a granddaughter of Col. John Reid who fought during the war of 1812, and who was then owner of the historic farm . . . .

23 October 1921: [The Rambler returned to the Ballard farm to visit the grave markers that had been set up in the meantime for 2 Union Generals who had been killed on the farm nearly the same time and within 200 yards of each other.] *In a little plot of ground 20 x 20 ft. bound by a single rail of two-inch galvanized iron pipe . . . are two big pieces of granite—about 2 feet wide, a foot and a half thick and 3 feet tall. Each bears a bronze tablet on its north face. 'Maj. Gen. Phillip Kearny, killed on this spot Sept. 1, 1862. The Tribute of Kearny's First New Jersey Brigade and friends.' The other reads: 'Maj. Gen. Isaac Ingalls Stevens with the flag of the Republic in his dying grasp, Sept. 1, 1862.'*

VIII-78
Chantilly, Va., Gen. Kearny Marker, 1921
[These markers appear the same today in the same plot on the southwest corner of West Ox Road and Monument St. in the Fairfax County Park Authority's "Ox Hill Battlefield Park."]

[No Rambler article concerning Manassas, the seat of Prince William County since 1893, was located. However, *Virginia, A Guide to the Old Dominion*[11] gives an introduction that would be appropriate for the Rambler's time: "Manassas [is] one long business street, several blocks of closely built houses and stores, and a wide outer fringe of well-spaced dwellings on landscaped lawns that lend a suburban atmosphere. . . . Manassas has grown from a railroad junction, which gave its name to two battles, into a trading center for a populous farming area."]

VIII-79
Manassas, Va., Street, 1921

VIII-80

Court House, Manassas, Va., 1921 [was completed in 1893]

Left: VIII-81

Court House, Entrance, Manassas, Va., 1921

VIII-82

Group at Court House Door, Clerk of the Court, Deputy and Crandell Mackey

VIII-83

Manassas, Railroad Station, 1915

VIII-84

Manassas, Va., Eastern College, 1921

VIII-85

Manassas, Va., The Presbyterian Church, 1921

VIII-86
Manassas
Confederate Monument

VIII-87
Manassas
Jubilee Memorial, In Court House Square
["In Commemoration of Manassas National Jubilee of Peace. The first instance in history where survivors of a great battle met 50 years after and exchanged friendly greetings at the place of mutual combat. Here on July 21, 1911, the closing scene was enacted.
THE TABLEAU OF THE UNITED STATES. The President, the Gov. of Va. and 48 maidens in white took part with 1,000 veterans of the blue and gray and 10,000 citizens of the New America." Unveiled 30 September 1915]

VIII-88

Country Store

[The sign over the door says: "C. C. Leachman
dealer in General Mdse. & Country Produce."
In Hill's 1906 *Virginia Business Directory and
Gazetteer*, p. 951, C. C. Leachman in Prince
William Co. is listed under General Stores
as being from Wellington, population 25, on
So. Ry.; 6 miles from Manassas C. H.]

Footnotes on Chapter VIII

1. Rambler, 8 November 1914.
1a. Frank W. Gapp, *The Commordore and the Whale,*
    Vantage Press, 1996, p. 18.
2. Connie P. and Mayo S. Stuntz, *This Was Tysons
    Corner, Virginia,* Privately Printed, 1990,
    Chap. 13.
2a. Ibid., p. 29.
3. Ibid., pp. 73–77.
4. Connie P. and Mayo S. Stuntz, *This Was Vienna,
    Virginia,* Privately Printed, 1987, p. 21.
5. Ibid., pp. 98–99.
6. Ibid., Chap. 2.
7. Ibid., Chap. 5.
8. Eugenia B. Smith, *Centreville, Va. Its History and
    Architecture,* Fairfax Board of Supervisors and
    Fairfax History Comm., 1973, p. 31.
9. Ibid., pp. 93–94.
10. Ibid., pp. 79–81.
11. WPA, p. 402.

Index

Calvert, Helen Chapman, Miss, *28*
Calvert, Susan Pearson Alexander, Mrs., 28, *28*
Canal, George Washington, *185, 186*
Carlyle House, *38*
Carlyle, John, *38*
Carper family, 190
Carper House, *190*
Carper's school, 191
Carpers Hill Road, *191*
Carpers Hill, 190
Carter, Mary Walker, 245
Carter, Robert (Councillor), 132, 134
Cemetery at Balls Bluff, *225*
Centerville (Bull Run), *276*
Centerville Episcopal church, 276
Centerville Red House, 273
Centerville Street, 270
Centerville, *265, 266, 267, 268, 269,* 271, *277,* 278
Centreville Methodist Episcopal Church, 272
Centreville, 12, 266
Chain Bridge Road, 161, *165,* 243, 245
Chain Bridge, 12, 161, *162,* 163, 164, 167, 172, 183
Chancellorsville House, *143*
Chancellorsville, Virginia, 12, *136,* 137, *138, 140, 141,* 142, 144
Chantilly Battlefield, *290*
Chantilly village, 289
Chantilly, Virginia, 276, 287, *288*
Chapman, Helen Mary, 28
Charcoal Burners (Great Falls), *179*
Charlestown, West Virginia, *232*
Chatham, *114*
Chatham-Lacy House, *113*
Chesapeake and Ohio Canal, 16
Chesterbrook, 164
Chestnut Thicket, 199, *200*
Christ Church Graveyard, *49*
Christ Church, *43, 53*
Church hill, 206
Church Point, 124
Civil War signal station and stockade, 247
Clarendon, 17
Cline, F. H., *255*
Clydes Restaurant, *247*
Cobb, Josephine, Miss, 10
Cobble Stones (in Alexandria), *42*
Cobblestone Breaking (in Alexandria), *45*
Colchester Ferry, *89*
Colchester, Virginia, 88, 89
Coleman family, 206
Coleman House, 209

Coleman, James, 207
Coleman, Samuel, *207*
Collins, Sara, 55
Colonial Beach, 133
Colony of Virginia, 100
Columbia Historical Society, 10, 11, 12, 13
Columbia Pike, 26, *26*
Columbian exposition at Chicago, 153
Colvin run, 161
communication tower, *247*
Confederacy, 137, 276
Confederate Grave Markers, *49*
Confederate Monument (in Front Royal), *235*
Confederate Monument (in Alexandria), *40, 41*
Confederates, 291
Contemplation, *256*
Core, John, 248
Cornwallis, *158*
Cornwell, Jesse, *198*
Coton farm, 217, 220
Coton House of the Lees, *219*
Country Day School, *169*
County of Loudoun, 183
County of Prince William, 107
Cranford Memorial, 79
Crittenden, Mr., *48*
Cronk, Greenberry, Mr. and Mrs., *265*
Crossroads, 161
Cruse, Midshipman, (monument of), *23*
Crutchet Place (near Falls Church), *258*
Cub run, 278
Custis, Ann Randolph, 20
Custis, George Washington Parke, 19, 20
Custis, John Parke, 29
Custis, Martha, 61
Custis, Nellie (birthplace of), *30*
Custis, Nellie, 20, 29, 67
Custom House (Yorktown, Virginia), *156*
Cutts, Samuel H., 175
Daniels, Edward, Colonel, 81
Day, John T., Dr., 206, 210
Day, William B., Dr., 206, 210
Daysville (in Loudoun County), 210
Daysville, 161, 209, 210, 211
Deanwood, 189
Delano, Louis (Great Falls), *182*
Dent, James, *66*
Dettingen parish, *78*
Dickeys Road station, 188
Difficult run, 182, 183, *184,* 193, 197, 198
Dogan, Dora, *285*

Dogan, Lucinda, 284, *285, 286*
Dogan, Lucy Senseney, *285*
Dogan, Mollie, *285*
Dogue Creek, *66,* 72
Dower House, 178
Drane house, 205
Dranesville Hotel, 208
Dranesville M. E. Church South, 206
Dranesville Tavern, 12, *208*
Dranesville, 161, 205, 206, *207,* 209, 210, 212, *214*
Drovers' Rest, 167
dry plate negatives, 10
Dumfries House, *99*
Dumfries, Virginia, *99,* 100, 101, *102,* 103
Durham House, C. J. S., *195*
Durham, C. J. S., Mrs., 203
Eisenhower Drive, 18, 19
electric trolley line, 243
Elkins station, 188
Elkins, 189, 199
Ellis, Wade Hampton, Judge, 96
Ellsworth, Elmer E., Colonel, 176, 178
Engleside, *69*
Evening Star, 9, 12
Fairfax Arms, 88
Fairfax Chapter, DAR, 184
Fairfax City Regional Library, 12
Fairfax County Chamber of Commerce, *160, 242, 259*
Fairfax County Park Authority, *208, 291*
Fairfax County Public Library Photographic Archive, 12
Fairfax County, 88, 259
Fairfax County, Virginia (map of), *56, 160, 242, 259*
Fairfax Court House, 243, 250, 257, 259, *260, 261, 262, 263, 264,* 276, 287
Fairfax History Commission, 10
Fairfax Town Cemetery, *263*
Fairfax village, 178, 183
Fairfax, Virginia, 12
Fairfax, Bryan, *53,* 196
Fairfax, Elizabeth Lindsay, 95
Fairfax, Henry (tomb of), *95*
Fairfax, Henry, 95, 96
Fairfax, John Walter, Colonel, 95
Fairfax, Jonathan, *95*
Fairfax, Sarah, *95*
Fairfax, William, 72
Fairfaxes of Belvoir, *73*